School Songs
and Gymslips

is to be returned on or before
last da~~te stamped below.~~

D0539982

School Songs and Gymslips

Grammar Schools
in the 1950s and 1960s

Marilyn Yurdan

Cover illustrations and throughout © Gwen Burns.

First published 2012

The History Press
The Mill, Brimscombe Port
Stroud, Gloucestershire, GL5 2QG
www.thehistorypress.co.uk

Typesetting and origination by The History Press
Printed in Great Britain
Manufacturing managed by Jellyfish Print Solutions Ltd

Contents

Foreword

School Songs and Gymslips is more than just the memories of a group of friends. It is a charming piece of social history which serves as an amusing reminder of how different life was in those days. Despite covering a period only just over fifty years ago it seems like a different world. I went to Holton Park Grammar School in the 1970s and during my time there it changed from a girls' grammar school to a co-educational comprehensive, but this book brings back so many memories – from sherbet fountains to Corona, from Tommy Steele to *Z Cars*, from stodgy puddings to Vesta curries; and that's not to mention the education. How different from today's world of the internet, yet children now will have their favourite teachers and the not so favourite, will still try to find ways out of doing homework and will still make lifelong friendships at school. This is an affectionate reminder of our schooldays, which I am sure will be enjoyed by anyone who wants to bring back the memories of what are always called the happiest days of our life.

The Rt Hon Theresa May MP
Home Secretary and Minister for Women and Equalities
2011

Acknowledgements

Special thanks to Kevin Heritage and Nigel Phillips of Wheatley Park School for making the school archives available to me and for their help and encouragement.

My grateful thanks, too, for their personal contributions to Marion Arnold, Peter Arnold (my 'mole from Lord Bill's'), Rosemary Boardman, Lucy Comerford, Judith Curthoys, Frances Dodds, Elizabeth Drury and Janet Eaton, and to schoolmates Patricia Harding, Stephanie Jenkins, Catherine Lorigan, Kath Mulligan, Carol Price, Jane Skinner, Ruth Pimm, Helen Sweet, Barbara Tearle and Margaret Wellens. Thanks (but no thanks) to 'the boys' who offered their services but did not qualify as wearers of gymslips.

Lastly, I must express my gratitude to the Rt Hon Theresa May MP, for giving up her valuable time to write a foreword to the book.

The reminiscences in this book, flattering and otherwise, are those of the individual contributors regarding the schools as they were seen in the 1950s and '60s, and are unlikely to be relevant to the schools as they are today.

Author's Note

Sources
Ministry of Education Report by HM's Inspectors undertaken
    6, 7, 8 and 9 December 1955, issued 10 March 1956
The National Grammar Schools Association (NGSA)
    www.ngsa.org.uk
Oxford Mail, various dates
Oxford Times, various dates

Abbreviations

Cheney	Oxford Girls'/Cheney School, Oxford
Chichester	Chichester High School for Girls, West Sussex
Cirencester	Cirencester Grammar School, Gloucestershire
Eccles	Eccles Grammar School, Eccles, Manchester
Fairfield	Fairfield Grammar School, Bristol
Holton	Holton Park Girls' Grammar School
Ilford	Ursuline High School, Ilford, Essex
Ilkley	Ilkley Grammar School, Ilkley, West Yorkshire

Littlemore	Littlemore Grammar School, Oxford
LWGS, or Lord Bill's	Lord Williams's Grammar School, Thame, Oxfordshire
Middleton	Queen Elizabeth's Grammar School, Middleton, Greater Manchester
Report	Ministry of Education report, 1955
Plymouth	Plymouth High School for Girls, Devon
Southgate	Southgate County Grammar School, Cockfosters, Greater London
South Shields	South Shields Grammar School, Tyne & Wear
Tollington	Tollington School, Muswell Hill, London
Tonbridge	Tonbridge Girls' Grammar School, Kent
Walthamstow	Walthamstow County High School, London E17
Wellingborough	County High School, Wellingborough, Northants

Introduction

This book started off being about the experiences of a group of pupils at Holton Park, a girls' grammar school in Oxfordshire, between 1958 and 1963. Before long, however, it had expanded to include those of girls from sixteen other grammar schools all over the country and now covers the period approximately 1955 to 1965. The information was obtained by sending out a set of questions, but the results are by no means a serious educational study. Rather, they are a light-hearted investigation as to how typical our own experiences had been.

The way that we got into grammar school was by passing the Eleven Plus examination, otherwise known as the scholarship, which had been introduced under the terms of the 1944 Education Act. In theory, everyone took it during their final year at primary school, but it would seem that those who definitely wouldn't be going to grammar school didn't turn up for it. This might be for a variety of reasons, the main ones being on religious or economic grounds.

The exam was taken soon after your eleventh birthday with the aim of ascertaining what type of secondary education you'd be best suited to. In theory there were three types – grammar, secondary modern or technical school – but in practice very few local authorities provided the last. Those of us who sat the exam had very little, if any, idea of the differences between these types of education as it was never explained to us in any shape or form. If we didn't get through, we went to the secondary modern, but there had been no indication of the seriousness of the results of this exam and how it would change our lives forever. Someone claimed that one day they were just told to go into the classroom and take an exam without even knowing what it was.

The Eleven Plus was in three parts: arithmetic (few children of this age had done decimals) and problem solving; English, including an essay and comprehension test; and general knowledge. There were different ways of announcing the results (pass, fail or borderline), the most compassionate being to send them to the pupils' fathers through the post, the worst being to announce them publicly at the end of morning assembly.

In some areas, passing the exam was not the end of the ordeal for the next step was a selection interview. Elsewhere, some girls passed the exam only to be informed that there was no place for them at grammar school. Some successful pupils were given a choice of grammar schools, in one case three, to which they were allowed to go.

In our own school's catchment area there was no further selection process and no alternative school. The only time that an interview was necessary was when a candidate was judged borderline, in which case they had to come to the school for the headmistress to assess them in person. At least two of our intake were borderline cases; one duly turned up for the interview and was accepted, the other came down with both mumps and measles a couple of days beforehand and was accepted *in absentia*, with only a courtesy visit to meet the head and buy items of uniform from the school office.

The great majority of grammar schools in existence at this time were assimilated into the comprehensive system by the early 1970s, when the school became part of a comprehensive on the same site. Today there are 164 state grammar schools in England and sixty-nine in Northern Ireland, but no state ones in either Scotland or Wales. The local authorities which have the most grammar schools are Kent with thirty-four, Lincolnshire with fifteen and Buckinghamshire with thirteen.

Modern grammar schools are secondary state schools, the only ones that are legally permitted to decide on their pupils for their academic ability. As they receive state funding, grammar schools don't charge fees for tuition but will charge for boarding if this is provided.

The primary schools from which my class came were nearly all small village ones, although a couple of us had been at a convent school. A report made by the Ministry of Education in 1955 defined the catchment area from which pupils came as 'a sparsely populated rural area' extending a dozen or so miles to the foot of the Chilterns and about 4 miles to the north and west. Pupils came from about twenty-five different primary schools. Over 80 per cent came to school by bus, the furthest away having a journey of more than 14 miles.

The report also stated that 'The area does not produce a large number of pupils of Grammar School calibre', so there was the dilemma of whether to go for an academic school or a full one! It went on to say that 'If the school is to remain full it is necessary to admit a proportion of girls with relatively little academic ability'.

This then was the school to which we were heading as we boarded the blue, double-decker bus that fine September morning in 1958.

One

Yesterday's Gone, Chad and Jeremy, 1964

So what is or was a grammar school? That depends on what era we are talking about. They fall into several categories: medieval; Tudor or Stuart; late nineteenth and twentieth century; and present day. Some are of hybrid foundation, including those that started off as being boys only and admitted girls later.

The earliest schools date from the sixth century and were those attached to monasteries and cathedrals. There, young boys were taught Latin grammar for entry into the Church and additional subjects that might be considered useful. Later, grammar schools were typically founded by a local benefactor, such as a clergyman or a merchant, for local boys. Pupils would stay at school until they were 14 and then go on to university or into posts in the Church.

Some schools in fact acted as preparatory schools for Oxford and Cambridge, with which they had a close affinity, while others were founded by private benefactors or guilds. All of the grammar schools founded in medieval and Tudor times admitted only boys until the last century, and some of them remain single sex to this day.

In the sixteenth century, as part of the Reformation, the majority of cathedral and monastic schools were suppressed and new ones opened in their place, paid for by money obtained from the Dissolution of the Monasteries. Both Edward VI and his sister Queen Elizabeth were supporters of grammar schools, which is the reason that so many schools bear their names. Towards the end of the nineteenth century, grammar schools became part of the system of secondary education throughout the United Kingdom apart from in Scotland, which had its own system. Over the years, some grammar schools were transformed into public schools that charged fees.

The percentage of places available at grammar schools in England and Wales for those who did not have to pay increased from about 33 per cent in 1913 to almost 50 per cent by 1937. After the 1944 Education Act, all secondary education in state schools was free and entry by examination only. Former fee-payers were allowed to continue at grammar school, but no more were accepted. When the tripartite (three-tiered) system of state-funded education was introduced, grammar schools became the selective section in England and Wales from the mid-1940s to the late 1960s. The other tiers were the secondary modern schools and the third technical ones, although these were few and far between. With the spread of the comprehensive system in the late 1960s and early '70s, some grammar schools opted out of the state system and charged fees. Others were abolished, but most were incorporated into comprehensive schools.

Queen Elizabeth's Grammar School, Middleton (formerly in Lancashire, now Greater Manchester), is the successor to Middleton Grammar School, the founder of which was Thomas Langley, Prince Bishop of Durham from 1406 until 1437 and three times Lord Chancellor of England. This originated in the Chantry School of Our Lady and St Cuthbert within St Leonard's parish church, which Langley built in 1412 as part of the rebuilding of the church. In 1572 Queen Elizabeth I granted the school letters patent and it took its present name. About 1586, the Chantry School was replaced by what is now the Old Grammar School, paid for by Alexander Nowell, Dean of St Paul's Cathedral and an old boy of the original school. A governing body was formed in 1910 with council input. The foundation governors still have control of monies given by ex-pupils and teachers to benefit children of Middleton who wish to go on to higher education. In the 1960s the headmaster was John Charles Edward Wren, a descendant of the more famous Sir Christopher. It became a high school in 1969.

Cirencester, in Gloucestershire, had a medieval grammar school dating back to about 1461. In 1881 its successor, the grammar school in Victoria Road, was opened and in the following year The Old School premises in Park Street were sold. This building is still known as The Old School. The grammar school closed in July 1966, when education in Gloucestershire was reorganised, and that September it merged with Deer Park Secondary Modern School to become what is now Cirencester Deer Park School. When all the pupils had been transferred to Deer Park, the old school's Victoria Road buildings were kept such as they were and are now the home of Cirencester County Junior School. Two of Cirencester Grammar School's best-known old boys are cricketer Wally Hammond (1903–65), who left at 17 to play for Gloucestershire, and Edward Jenner (1749–83), the pioneer of vaccination.

Andover Grammar School, Hampshire, began with a London merchant named John Hanson, who held the position of bailiff (or chief magistrate) of Andover. When he retired from office in 1569 he gave £200 to found a free school for the boys of the town and paid the fees of its master. This school, which opened in 1571 near St Mary's church, came to be known as Andover Grammar School. It became part of the comprehensive system in 1974 when a new school, the John Hanson Community School, was formed, thus honouring Hanson four centuries after the opening of his original school.

The only boys' grammar school in this book, Lord Williams's at Thame has been included for several reasons: it was one of the traditional grammar schools, not a modern version, and it possesses a 1575 copy of its statutes so that we know exactly how a Tudor grammar school functioned. Lord Williams's Grammar School, Thame, Oxfordshire (affectionately known for generations as Lord Bill's), was the male equivalent of Holton Park. It is now a mixed sports and community college called Lord Williams's School.

The foundation and subsequent history of Lord Bill's, along with its community ethos, are worth examining as it was a genuine grammar school, typical of the category from which many of today's public schools evolved and on which the later so-called grammar schools were modelled. Many of the features of such boys' schools were also copied by the twentieth-century girls' grammar schools, which are the subject of this book. It was founded according to the terms of the will of Lord John Williams, Baron Williams of Thame, who died in 1559 and was housed in Church Road. Among its alumni are the patriot John Hampden; two regicides, Sir Richard

Ingoldsby and Simon Mayne, who signed Charles I's death warrant; John Fell, Dean of Christchurch Cathedral and Bishop of Oxford; and the Orientalist Edward Pocock.

We are able to discover exactly what went on in an Elizabethan grammar school thanks to the survival of a very rare copy of its statutes (and other documents) called *Schola Thamensis*, which was printed in London in 1575. The statutes take up twenty-eight of its fifty-five pages and are a mine of information about the day-to-day life of the school. We know, for instance, that the first day's teaching was on 29 November 1570 under headmaster Edward Harris, who remained in post until 1597 and was buried a few hundred yards away in the parish church of St Mary the Virgin. Here, his headless brass effigy can still be seen, very close to Lord Williams himself.

Boys started there at the age of 7, by which age they were expected to be able to read and write. Like most Elizabethan schools, they attended for nine or ten hours a day, from six until eleven in the morning, with a break for lunch, and then again from one until five in the winter (when they had to bring their own candles for dark evenings) and until six in the summer. They had a day free during the week plus feast days and four annual holidays, each one just over two weeks long.

Living up to its title, all teaching at Lord Williams's was in Latin and this was the only subject in the curriculum. It was a free grammar school in the sense that there was no charge for tuition, but there were charges of 8*d* on admission. This was spent on books, while a further 2*d* a quarter went on cleaning and 'to the purchasing of rods'. However, any boy who lived in the town and those who could claim 'Founder's kin' paid nothing apart from 1*s* each quarter to the master and sixpence to the usher.

The school day started and finished with a religious service, with prayers in Latin and its own Latin hymn. In addition, a passage from the Bible was read before dinner and the boys were obliged to go to St Mary's on Sundays and on religious festivals. They had to sit in the chancel along with the inmates of Lord Williams's almshouses, adjacent to the school.

Like many similar schools, Lord Bill's went into a decline, in this case in the first half of the eighteenth century when masters were more interested in lining their pockets than educating their charges. By 1866 Thame Grammar School had only two day pupils and not a single boarder. A new and dynamic board of governors was appointed in 1873 with the target of setting up a renewed school which would cater for up to 120 pupils, half of which were to board. It was suggested that the ancient school building be extended and even that the historic almshouses be demolished. In the event a new school was constructed on the Oxford Road, although it failed to attract as many pupils as had been hoped. After the turn of the century, however, the situation picked up and it went from strength to strength. In 1974 it went comprehensive when it combined with the recently opened Wenman School.

The foundation of Ilkley Grammar School, West Yorkshire, dates back to 1607, when it was decided the sum of £100, which had been left to the town by resident George Marshall, should be used to maintain a grammar school and master in Ilkley. It wasn't until 1636, however, that the schoolhouse was erected in Addingham Road. In 1696, Reginald Heber of Hollin Hall left a further £200 that, with other money, was used to buy land to be rented out. The vicar of the parish church was responsible for hiring and paying the master, something which was to cause considerable contention over the next 200 years. An inspection carried out in 1866 was less than flattering and it was forced to close eight years later, when the pupils were transferred to the new National School in Leeds Road. Nevertheless, the idea of an independent grammar school persisted, and in 1872 a board of governors nominated by the schools' inspector broke away from the church and put forward the suggestion of a new building. After a considerable amount of arguing over the following two decades, the present school was opened in 1893 in Cowpasture Road.

Cheney Girls' School, Headington, Oxford, can claim to be the oldest girls' school in the city. Before moving to its Headington site in 1959, it had occupied at least four others. Its origins lay in the late eighteenth century as a Baptist Sunday school in Oxford. By 1812, however, it had become the co-educational United Charity and Sunday school and was situated in Gloucester Green. It then moved to St Ebbes in 1824, and ten years later it became a single-sex girls' school, which went by the name of the Penson's Gardens Girls' British School. The Oxford school board took responsibility for it in 1898, and in 1901 it was renamed yet again as the Oxford Central Girls' School and moved to New Inn Hall Street. The new school building that it used is now part of St Peter's College. In 1959 the Central moved to its present site in Headington, when its name was changed to Cheney Girls' Grammar School. It merged with the neighbouring Cheney Technical School when Oxford went comprehensive in 1972.

One day in the 1920s, when my mother was at the Central, she was told by the rather formidable headmistress that she should sit the School Certificate examinations, the forerunners of O levels. In those days candidates had to pay to take the exams and my mother was sent back home in the dinner hour to fetch the amount required. Her mother impressed upon her the need to take this seriously and not to waste the money. The girl hastily agreed, anxious to get back to school and hand over the money to the head. When the time came to sit the exams, which were held in the intimidating University of Oxford Examination Schools, she hadn't given them much thought, let alone read the set book, one of which she remembers as being *Ivanhoe*. Needless to say, when she looked at the questions she was unable to write more than her name. The next day she again presented herself, went into the exam room and sat down at a desk. When she asked for paper and writing equipment, she was told that she wasn't supposed to be taking that exam, so she left and spent the afternoon in the Botanic Garden nearby. When the results came out they were displayed in Blackwell's Bookshop in Broad Street, where candidates had to go to find out how they'd done. She didn't bother, and nobody, either at school or at home, mentioned it again.

The origins of Holton Park Girls' Grammar School, Wheatley, Oxfordshire, lay in a large private school for girls, which opened in 1849 next door to the Wesleyan Chapel. In 1877 it changed its name to the Girls' Grammar School when it moved into the buildings in Church Road, which had recently been vacated by Lord Williams's Grammar School. In 1908 it moved again, this time to the larger site that had been occupied by the Oxford County School for Boys, the mansion and the former town house of the Norreys family. It was recognised as a secondary school and until 1921 received a subsidy from the Oxfordshire Education Committee. In 1917 there were seventy-seven boarders but in 1943 it stopped taking boarders. From 1921 onwards it accepted only 'county scholars' from Oxfordshire and Buckinghamshire and by the time it closed in 1948 there were 110 of these, plus thirty private fee-payers and thirty-five younger pupils in its preparatory school.

In September 1948 the girls went to a temporary secondary school opened by the local education authority in Water Eaton Manor. This school had 132 pupils, including a preparatory class of 10-year-olds. There were ten girls in the fifth year, but there was no sixth form. The move to Holton Park, near Wheatley, took place the following June and, once there, the numbers rose until in 1955 there were 171 pupils, of which eighteen were in the sixth form.

An example of a boys' school that became co-educational is Fairfield Grammar School, a Bristol secondary school founded in 1898 as Fairfield Secondary and Higher Grade School. In 1945 it was given grammar school status, but closed in 2000 when a new comprehensive, Fairfield High School, opened on the same site. This later moved to Stottbury Road, Bristol.

Eccles Secondary School was the first secondary school built by Lancashire County Council after the 1902 Education Act. Its foundation stone was laid by Alderman Sir Henry Fleming Herbert, the chairman of the county education committee, in 1910, and the first intake of about ninety-five pupils started there on 18 September 1911. In 1944 the school changed its name to Eccles Grammar School and fees were abolished. Probably the school's most famous old boy is Tony Simpson, better known as Tony Warren, the creator of *Coronation Street*. In 1973 it combined with Ellesmere Park Secondary School to become Ellesmere Park High School.

The Roman Catholic Ursuline High School in Ilford (formerly Essex, but now Greater London) was founded by the Ursuline order of nuns in 1903 and has been catering for the local community in Ilford ever since. It is now a science college, Catholic Voluntary Aided School for Girls.

Plymouth High School for Girls had its origins in the Devon and Cornwall Girls' School Company, which was formed in 1874. The company opened a school for girls in the September of that year in a temporary home, Sherwell House, North Hill, Plymouth. A fund had already been set up to raise money to buy a site and the first section of the new school was opened nearby by the Bishop of Exeter, Doctor Frederick Temple, in 1878. It remained a fee-paying school until after the Education Act of 1944.

In 1890 Walthamstow County High School for Girls in Greater London was opened on Church Hill, by a committee of subscribers as a private school. Its first venue was in the schoolroom of Trinity church in West Avenue, but a few months later it relocated to Church Hill House. By 1906, when there were 108 girls and four boys in the school, the teaching was said to be 'excellent and cultivated'. In 1911 Essex County Council took responsibility for the school and two years later it moved into new premises on the old vicarage glebe. Major extensions to the school took place in 1918, 1928 and 1962.

Tonbridge County School in Kent opened in January 1905 in the Technical Institute in Avebury Avenue with nineteen pupils. It was Mrs Taylor, the first headmistress, who adopted the school motto 'Courage and Honour'. In 1913 the school relocated to the School on the Hilltop. The Education Act of 1944 turned the County School into the County Grammar School for Girls, for pupils who passed the newly introduced Eleven Plus exam. New buildings and facilities were added from the 1950s onwards, ending with the redevelopment of the original School on the Hilltop, which was completed in June 2010.

Southgate School in Enfield, Greater London, began life in 1907 as Southgate County School, at Broomfield House, Palmers Green. Later it moved to Fox Lane, then in 1967, it combined with Oakwood Secondary Modern School in Chase Road, Southgate. The Fox Lane site closed in 1960 and a new one was bought in Cockfosters.

The County High School, Wellingborough, was also founded in 1907 in a large Victorian house named The

Lindens, with a Miss Tinkler as its first headmistress. The school was actually set up by the governors of Wellingborough School, the local public school, as a result of the 1902 Education Act. The school moved to its new buildings in 1912; these now form part of Wrenn School. In 1975 the girls' County High School went 'co-ed' when it was merged with Wellingborough Grammar School for boys.

In 1936 the new South Shields Girls' High School, Tyne and Wear, was opened in the premises recently vacated by the boys of Westhoe Higher Grade School, when the new High School for Boys opened in Lisle Road.

The first school on the site of what would become Tollington Grammar School in Islington, North London, was a private boys' school, Tollington School. After the Second World War the school became a state grammar school, with the former preparatory school adjacent becoming Tetherdown Primary School. In 1958 the grammar school changed sites with the Girls' High School, which had been in existence since 1910. The present school was built in the same year and the High School for Girls and Tollington Grammar School for Boys combined to become the co-educational Tollington Grammar School. When the borough of Haringey went comprehensive in 1967, Tollington Grammar merged with next-door neighbour the William Grimshaw Secondary Modern School, to form the present Creighton School.

Littlemore Grammar School in Oxford was one of the shortest lived, lasting a mere ten years. It was opened in 1958 with Mr Ben Halliday (known as 'Doc') as its first headmaster. He managed to make some headway with the new institution but before long the comprehensive system was introduced and the grammar school was combined with its next-door neighbour, Northfield Secondary Modern, and the new Peers School opened in 1968.

There were quite significant differences between grammar schools in the 1950s and '60s and it's not likely that this following experience was unique:

In 1963 I moved from South Shields to Oxford – feeling pretty scared as Oxford was 'the seat of learning' and I thought that I would be so far behind in my year. How different could it have been? The school was co-ed, uniform quite pretty and education way below standard of my previous school. So much so that I spent a lot of time sitting at the back of the class reading! The girls did not like netball or hockey but did like the boys! In my opinion Littlemore Grammar School ruined my chances of good employment by the lack of discipline and 'thirst' for learning. I could not wait to leave.

This is the definition of today's grammar schools from the website of the National Grammar Schools Association (www. ngsa.org.uk/index.php):

Grammar schools are state secondary schools. They are the only state schools in England (where there are 164) and Northern Ireland (where there are 69) that are allowed by law to select all their pupils on the grounds of high academic ability. There are no state grammar schools in Scotland or Wales. Because they are funded by the state, grammar schools do not charge fees, though a few grammar schools have boarding facilities. They will charge fees for boarding, but not for tuition.

Of the schools featured in this book, only Plymouth High School for Girls and Tonbridge Grammar School for Girls remain grammar schools.

Perhaps the last word on former grammar schools should be that of the Vicar of Flixton, the Reverend F.R. Cooke, who said, 'Maybe the time has come for the school to die, as education in this country enters a new stage. But if what Eccles Grammar School stood for in education dies then something very valuable will have died in England.'

Two

Walk Right In, The Rooftop Singers, 1963

The first day finally did arrive and it coincided with the local fair, which took over the entire main street of our town. This meant that the school bus wasn't able to reach the town hall, the usual picking-up point, so that we had to make our way to the end of the fair to catch it. To this day any mention of the start of the autumn term conjures up images of broken coconuts waiting in the gutter for the less fastidious to pounce on and put in their satchels with squeaks of joy. Boxer dogs, Dalmatians and German Shepherds guarded caravans, apparently dozing, but one wary brown eye always on the alert. Showmen's children (lucky, lucky kids) queued at the special standpipes, which had been put up to supply the vans with water. Above all, there was the smell of used cooking oil and cold fried onions combined with wafts of stale beer, which gave the fair its particular aroma; in short, all the glamour of the morning after the night before.

The new girls, half a dozen or so of us – a couple from a convent, two from a nearby village and the rest from the local primary school – were all decked out in navy and bright gold. We stood around awkwardly in self-conscious contrast to the old hands, strapping 14- and 15-year-olds who sported dull gold braid on their blazers and wore skirts rubbed shiny by terms of misuse. Suddenly, the crisp newness of our uniforms became undesirable, branding us as outsiders with a lot to learn. Then there were the real seniors, the sixth-formers, including the head girl who had a gold tassel on her beret to distinguish her from lesser scholars.

We tried, unsuccessfully, to intrude ourselves into the lower deck of the 'Blue B' – the elderly double-decker that wheezed and groaned its way along the 7 miles to school each morning. The lower deck was the territory of the previous year's occupants, and they certainly were not prepared to welcome new arrivals. 'Perhaps they can't go upstairs,' I overheard, 'maybe they get travel sick.' We crept upstairs out of their way and into the province of the third and fourth years, although the head girl was up there as well, sitting in isolation on the front seat. All the others were exchanging news and views about their summer activities, and we felt very small fish indeed.

On the outskirts of the town we were startled by a sudden outburst of activity and shrieks. It seemed as if every one of our neighbours had rushed to one side of the bus, until it must surely overturn and crush us all. Then the racket ceased as abruptly as it had begun, they resumed their places and talent-spotting at the boys' grammar school was over until the return journey.

The rest of the way was uneventful and it was with mixed feelings that we turned into the school drive and were soon at the old stables. Here, other vehicles were disgorging their loads. Local girls, on foot or on bicycles, threaded their way through the mass of bodies, with lots of shouting and ringing of bike bells. It was all very bewildering, and at least one of us would have willingly got straight back on the bus. There was nobody around to direct us and tell us even in which direction to start off, so we followed on behind the rest. New arrivals today, whether at school or university, should be grateful for the 'buddies' scheme, by which older students adopt new ones and make sure they settle in and things run smoothly for the first couple of days at least.

Once inside the school building, we somehow managed to find the right classroom, Room D, where we were greeted by our form mistress, a mild-mannered spinster of uncertain age who clucked over her charges the minute they arrived. She was one of the maths teachers, and must have learnt from bitter experience to make the best of them until they turned on her, as class after class of their predecessors had done over the years that she'd been teaching.

The thirty or so of us spent the first half of the morning collecting exercise books in a dazzling range of colours, some for 'rough' work, others for 'best'. The girls in the front row were given a pile of books to pass backwards, and, as the collection grew, shy, sympathetic glances and remarks were exchanged with neighbours sitting in front and behind. After the mid-morning break, when we had disposed of our luke-warm and slightly smelly milk, it was back to Room D for the distribution of textbooks and a series of homilies concerning privileges and obligations.

At last the dinner bell (nothing so refined as lunch with us), and a somewhat basic meal eaten from trestle tables. This was only the first of many hundredweight of shepherd's pies, boiled beef and carrots, salads, dried fruit, semolina, assorted

tarts and, above all, stodge masquerading as sponge puddings, which we would be required to consume over the next
five years. Each table was presided over by a junior prefect, an
unfortunate fifth-former whose duty it was to dole out equal
portions and ensure that no one got away with less than the
others did. Well primed and rehearsed, they tried to encourage enthusiasm by the time-honoured method of telling us
how grateful little black children of unspecified national-
ity would be to receive such a feast. Another ploy was to
attempt to impress upon us what an essential role prunes and
watery pink custard could play in improving the constitution
of a growing girl. Neither method was successful.

All this, however, was in the future. That first day we sat,
six to a table, positioned at the bottom of the main staircase, well away from the certain corruption, ribald remarks
and lamentable table manners of our elders. After clearing
away our own tables and benches, we were turned out into
the school grounds where we roamed around aimlessly, smil-
ing hopefully at any face we chanced to recognise above the
tell-tale new uniform.

When the long, long day was over, we felt that we had
made a considerable amount of progress and didn't even
flinch when the Blue B lurched past the boys' school again.
We felt good. We now knew what to expect from our new
lives. Unbelievable as it would have seemed only hours ago,
we felt that we would ourselves eventually become cool
second years surveying a fresh batch of nervous newcomers.

All the teaching, apart from art, gym and obviously games,
was done inside 'the House', now known as 'the Old House'.
There were classrooms on both floors; the larger ones upstairs
were the former bedrooms. These had adjoining small dressing rooms (called 'divisional rooms' in the 1955 Ministry of
Education report), also used for teaching. At this early date

we were unaware of the House's haunted reputation, and in any case it was not at all creepy, in fact quite the reverse, being in the Georgian style with white paintwork, sash windows with shutters and crystal knobs, marble fireplaces and high ceilings.

On the first floor at the north-east corner of the building was Room A, the second-year form room. Overlooking the terrace, Room A contained the lending library of about 500 fiction books for the use of the junior forms. This consisted of the usual mind-improving classics – the great majority of which were in pristine condition – a few biographies and works on travel, natural history and the most popular titles: books about adventures in girls' schools. These were quite old-fashioned, even then, and the equivalent of the more numerous ones about boys' boarding schools. Most were from the *Chalet School* series by Elinor M. Brent-Dyer, which started in the 1920s; Enid Blyton's *Malory Towers* (now reprinted in a twenty-first-century format) and, best of all, the *Abbey* books by Elsie J. Oxenham – much more up-to-date as they were written in the 1940s and '50s. Part of the popularity of these books was due to the fact that, like us, the schoolgirl heroines went to school in ancient buildings where all manner of fascinating and scary discoveries awaited them.

Next along the corridor was Room B. The territory of the upper fifth and also overlooking the terrace, it was a nondescript little room packed with desks, which left room for nothing else. Room C, next door, was a small seminar-type room which was seldom used. Nearly opposite was an open archway at elbow level, which gave out on to the main staircase and was popular for leaning on to watch the world go by below. This has since been blocked up, presumably for safety reasons.

The bright and airy Room D, the home of first years, occupied the south-east corner and had a dual aspect, looking out on to the terrace and the south side of the House; it was probably the lightest and most welcoming room in the school. It adjoined the staff room, which would have been rather crammed for the number of teachers but as about half of them were part time or 'visiting', they were unlikely to use it all at the same time.

Next came Room E, belonging to the fourth years and overlooking the south side of the House. On one notable occasion an entire window frame went crashing down on to the southern terrace when someone in our class put pressure on a window which was sticking. Fortunately, there was nobody underneath at the time and the wrecker was herself unscathed as the glass didn't break until it hit the ground. Room F was another small seminar-type room, seldom used and overlooking the south side of the House, while Room G next to it was that holy of holies: the inner sanctum of the upper sixth.

The supposedly haunted marble front staircase ran down from outside these rooms, off the southern corridor to the front porch, and was decorated by examples of 'outstanding' artwork by the pupils. Above the staircase was (and still is) a glass dome, the light from which adds to the spacious feeling. The area under the stairs, where first years had their meal, adjoined a corridor from which led off the hall, the domestic science room, the laboratory and Room K. Aspiring painters also had their work framed and put on temporary display in the front porch, which was in fact a stone-paved vestibule that doubled up as a sick bay. Here there were three shelves, above each of which was a framed portrait of the three worthies after whom the school houses were named. The shelves held the various trophies won by members of the houses, and it was also the venue for the sale of buns brought up from

Wheatley Bakery. The fact that the front porch was another place used for first-form dinners, and so smelt of hot food (a little like Woolworth's) for an hour or two after the event, tended to detract somewhat from its dignity.

The hall, which overlooked the terrace, had several functions such as morning assembly, the serving of lunch and being the venue for music classes. It had been an imposing room in its day and still retained its old fireplace, above which was a wooden board displaying the names and details of pupils who had gained admittance to university. When we were there, the hall's appearance was somewhat marred by the trestle tables, benches and stacks of rather weary utility chairs, which leant against one wall in readiness for the next dinner time.

Next to the hall, the domestic science room, overlooking the terrace, saw cookery and needlework. It also served as a classroom for the lower fourth, the members of which had to use its cookery tables instead of desks and keep their belongings in a set of lockers across the corridor, under the back stairs. As a consolation prize, they were allowed to use the terrace as their own patio, which they usually reached by clambering out of the window.

The science lab also lined the terrace. It boasted stained and scratched benches (one of which was inscribed 'Elvis Forever'), and the usual assorted glassware, Bunsen burners, odd specimens in glass-fronted cupboards and fridges containing even odder stuff (such as deceased grass snakes). To finish it off, leeches fished out of the moat languished in a jar on the window sill. A series of rather suspect sinks under the windows hindered access to the terrace from the lab. Just the thought of the room brings back a malodorous mixture of memories: acrid fumes from gas burners and recent experiments, combined with that of formaldehyde and a faint whiff of general decay.

Like Room D, Room K – that of the third years – was on the south-east corner. With a dual aspect looking out on to the terrace and the south side of the House, it was a light and pleasant room with good views. It was also, however, spoilt by the lingering smell of naked fear induced by the verbal French tests which were held there. These were inflicted by the deputy head and took the form of 'last man standing', but in reverse. Victims started off with the whole class sitting while all manner of fairly obscure grammatical and vocabulary questions were fired at them. Those who failed to answer correctly were made to stand, but were allowed to take their seats again if they did better in a following round.

On the other side of the front door was the library, entered from the bottom of the back stairs. The 1955 Ministry of Education report mentions that there was no initial grant for books, but by 1955 there were nearly 2,000 purchased from an annual grant of about £80. In the early 1950s, timber from the site was sold and the money used to buy a complete set of encyclopaedias. The senior English mistress doubled up as librarian, helped by one of the older pupils. The room was small, with seating for only twenty-four readers. There were magazines and two newspapers to pay for, which girls contributed 6d a term to in the mid-1950s, although by the end of the decade this charge was dropped.

It was also used by O level music candidates, who would listen to their set records for examinations – a practice which invariably drew protests from the room's other users, especially when Beethoven or Wagner was on the turntable. For some unknown reason, the radiators in the library were chained to the walls – perhaps lest they be moved around or even stolen – and pupils were given dire warnings not to sit on them in cold weather as they'd develop piles (haemorrhoids). All in all, though, the library was a warm, clean room in which to chat and catch up. It was also the place to find out what was cool and what was not in the latest edition of *Honey* ('For the teens and twenties', or, by 1962, 'Young, gay and get-ahead'), *Romeo* and *Valentine*, or even the more childish *Girl* if there was a feature on one of our idols. We were usually left in peace to get on with it, but occasionally a group of prissy first years or trouble-making third-formers would report us for disturbing their studies and Auntie Dottie (more of her later) would burst in, breathing flames.

The back stairs, ordinary wooden affairs and very much 'downstairs', were built to reach the upper floor from the service areas. They ran between the landing outside the school office and Miss D.'s study and living accommodation to the area outside the hall. There was other living accommodation in this extension, notably that occupied by the deputy head.

A side door (known as the back door) was approached from the driveway leading from the stables and took you to the kitchens, cloakrooms and loos to the left, with the hall directly ahead, and off into the main downstairs corridor of House to the right. The clear glass in this door was replaced with the reinforced type after a fourth-former put her hand through it and, in so doing, bloodied both herself and the paintwork. A separate, modern block facing this door housed Rooms X and Y, two adjoining rooms used for dance, gym and painting, which were normally used as one larger Room Z. Often deposits of powder paints or trodden-in pastels were to be found on the floor, discovered only when you'd got them already about your person or all over your gym kit.

The grounds were very attractive and were invariably referred to as such in any account of the school, but of course were only a small part of the original estate. By 1958, apart from the buildings and the island, they consisted of the stables area, the driveway which skirted the island, the terrace, the dell, a hockey pitch and netball courts, which doubled up as tennis courts in the summer. There was a further grass tennis court that reverted to lawn in the winter; this was to be the site of the long-awaited swimming pool, which eventually appeared thanks to a concerted effort from pupils and parents. However, neither tennis court nor pool survives and the area has now reverted to being a plain stretch of grass.

A recurrent and fascinating theme during history periods throughout the school was the House's reputation for being haunted. During the late 1950s and in the '60s, the history teacher would tell the junior classes tales about the school ghosts. These anecdotes would not have been appreciated by the head, as they were rather vague and in no way related to any recognised examination syllabus.

When the estate changed hands towards the end of the eighteenth century, it included what had been a medieval manor house surrounded by a deep moat. Soon after he moved there the new owner realised that the old house was badly haunted and promptly had it demolished. He did this so thoroughly that not a single stone was left standing on another and it was assumed that this had got rid of the ghostly residents. Work then started on the present house: a castle in miniature with a lawn separating it from the moat. It was this house that was eventually converted into our school.

As far as we could gather, the ghosts included that of a nurse who, carrying a small boy in her arms, would run full tilt down the front stairs. The story went that the nurse had tripped while going down the stone staircase and had fallen on top of the child, crushing him to death. There were suggestions that the child had been buried under the site of the front hall of the present building, where the apparition is said to disappear, although the reasons for such a supposition were never given. A less frequent sight was a small dog said to trot along one of the upstairs corridor, but always avoiding capture.

One writer explained that when he was about 12 years old he was standing at the bottom of the front stairs, when he happened to look up and see a boy of about the same age running down the staircase as fast as he could possibly go. When he put out his arm to restrain him, the strange boy turned sharply round at the bottom of the stairs and rushed in the direction of the front hall. The watcher particularly noticed that the boy's feet did not touch the ground. When the strange boy reached the front hall, first his head and then his body 'went up suddenly in smoke, as if he had exploded' in the most alarming way. Another apparition is the 'very big woman' wearing a high-collared gown with puff sleeves, who has been seen in what was the butler's pantry. There are several versions of these sightings and one, of a brown lady, persists in the village to this day. Despite its being a brand-new building, one by one the servants handed in their notice and visitors who stayed in a certain bedroom began to complain about a sensation of unknown persons being in the room. These complaints came with an embarrassing frequency.

No one at the school in the time that we were there had heard of anyone who had personal experience of the ghosts, although few people spent much time there after four o'clock in the afternoon or at weekends. Nevertheless, we girls were taken with the idea of there still being resident ghosts on the premises. Perhaps it was just an old story made up to scare children, we decided, or perhaps there had once been ghosts but they'd been frightened away by the rock 'n' roll that now blasted out during wet lunch breaks, or by the thundering of 150 or so pairs of school shoes up and down the supposedly haunted staircase.

Three

All Dressed Up for School, The Beach Boys, 1964

We knew what our new uniform consisted of before we started at grammar school as we'd seen other girls wearing it in and around the town. The main items were a navy-blue, square-necked gymslip, white (originally Vyella) long-sleeved blouse and a blazer. Some items, such as the beret, blazer badges and the sash-type belt called a girdle, were bought from the school office, the rest from the local outfitters. Optional extras were a cardigan (not a jumper) and a rain-coat. At that age, our clothes had moved on from the 'age 10' stage but we still had chest measurements rather than busts. Most of us only had one gymslip each and they were washed, ironed and aired over the weekend. Underneath we wore plain white shirt-style blouses, navy school knick-ers (others had the 'famous green knickers') and compulsory vests. Navy was a popular colour for school uniforms, as was bottle green (both good 'dirt' colours); grey, maroon and brown were more unusual. Our school colours of navy and gold coincided with those of the most successful local football club, and during the school's first year one of the pupils was the daughter of the team's manager.

Gymslips were worn in our three junior forms, as at a number of other schools, with the change to skirts (or the occasional variation of a pinafore dress or bibbed skirt with crossover straps) coming in the fourth year. Some of the skirts were pleated, others straight or gored. Elsewhere, shirts were generally white, apart from one school where they had blue and white. Our ties were also navy, with a diagonal gold stripe. This was the part of the uniform which was most abused as they weren't washable and soon showed evidence of weeks of egg yolks, custard and gravy. Even worse, the fourth years, whose ties were on display once they'd graduated from gymslips to blouses and skirts, used to fray the edges of theirs.

When the school opened, gymslips were worn by all forms apart from the sixth. In our day, by the time the fifth form and sixth forms were reached new ties were in order, for this was the time of badges of office: junior and full prefects' badges; hockey, tennis and netball badges; and the ultimate accolade, the head girl's badge. Prefects also sported yellow ties and yellow tassels on their berets. Juniors of the first three years had to make do with house badges – round coloured ones in red, blue or green if they felt so inclined – but few did. Ties were worn at most schools, although there were a couple of exceptions, and most ties were striped. In some places the colour of the tie had its own significance and showed the wearer's status.

We wore cardigans, navy of course, with skirts but seldom with gymslips. We were allowed to wear navy winter coats and raincoats but these were very rarely seen, blazers being much preferred whatever the weather. The blazers had gold binding and a woven gold badge on the pocket, which showed what was supposed to be an image of the House surrounded by laurel leaves. At most schools blazers, jumpers (sometimes with a trim) and cardigans matched the colour of the gymslips and skirts; at others schools blazers were part of the summer uniform, coats and macs of the school's main colour being worn in the winter. One unusual jacket was 'a pretty, reddish pink and the winter skirt was the same colour as the jacket, with a shaped neckline'. Red, blue or red girdles (depending on the house the wearer was in), similar to the ones worn by our juniors, were to be found at one other school but were unusual. Scarves were striped in the school colours but not always worn.

Our winter headgear was a very ordinary navy beret adorned with a miniature version of the badge; most people wore the beret like a mushroom, but a more enlightened group of seniors pulled the front into a peak and sewed the badge on to the top of it so that it could still be seen. Variations on winter hats included a navy one with a grey stripy hat band, a plain green hat, a beret with a bobble and, at a school where they had hat inspections, a navy bucket hat with ribbons in school colours. The most unusual were a Juliet cap, a black velour number and the felt tricorn hat worn at a school in a coastal town to reflect the naval connection; this hat had to be worn even in summer when it was very hot.

We had to own a pair of stout, brown, all-weather outdoor shoes and a lighter indoor pair, also brown, with straps or laces – in practice usually some version of Clark's sandals. Everyone of a certain age, male and female alike, will doubtless remember the mixed feelings invoked by a pair of brand-new shoes, or, as was more likely, sandals. On one hand, there was the smart shiny newness of them, the smell of fresh leather and the strange, slightly heady odour given off by those crisp, white crepe soles when sniffed. The downside was the sore and rubbed toes, and the raw and bleeding heels, which the proud owner had to endure for a matter of weeks. Indeed, no sooner was the crepe discoloured and the leather broken in and comfortably scuffed, then our feet would have outgrown them and it would be time for a new pair, and the whole process would start all over again.

The walls of the corridor just outside Room A were adorned with grisly pictures showing what happened to teenage feet that had been sacrificed on the altar of high fashion, and how crippled and deformed they soon became. Luckily, all was not lost, however. If we wore Clark's sandals from babyhood, it seemed, all would be well with our feet for life! This proved to be totally incorrect when it came to one particular pair, which led to giant blisters that burst, became infected and, even when these had received medical treatment, continued to be tender for months afterwards. So much, we thought, for sensible shoes. In 1959 T-strap shoes came in and offered a stylish change from the traditional kids' sandals. They could be worn to school with either the regulation white socks or with stockings after hours. We were expected to change into indoor shoes as soon as we entered the building, not for comfort or merely to stop mud being trampled all over the building, but to preserve the ancient stairs and flagstones from desecration.

There was little deviation from white ankle socks, although a few schools wore grey ones and very unusual white and green ones have been reported. Those of the very highest rank were permitted to wear stockings on special occasions, but usually preferred socks because stockings and suspender belts were so uncomfortable (this was well before the arrival of tights); they were seldom worn if there was nobody present to impress. Stockings were more generally known as 'nylons', and by the time it was our turn to graduate from socks they were available without seams and were no longer 'fully fashioned'.

In those pre-tights days, uncomfortable stocking tops and seams would get completely out of control. Suspenders often came adrift from their belts, but could be replaced in an emergency with a sixpence. Beginners infuriated and frustrated by seamed stockings that crept sneakily round their legs (the discomfort worsened by a reaction to the metal of which the suspenders were made) would sometimes give up in disgust, take off their stockings and stuff them into their clutch bags. The only good thing about nylons was the fact that when one had become laddered beyond repair with nail varnish, it could be thrown away and its twin kept to match up with another of the same (or similar) shade.

Some of the names of the colours were very imaginative, but among the most fashionable were 'nude' and 'American tan'. Black stockings were reserved as part of the uniforms of nurses, policewomen and, of course, French maids! Fishnets were out of the question. The most popular brands were Aristoc, Charnos, Bear Brand and Pretty Polly. Every hosiery department had disembodied leg-shaped models resting atop cabinets, displaying the colour and thickness of the merchandise. Nylons came in packets of a pair of singles, and it was some time into the tights era before multi-packs became common. If nylons were kept for any length of time before being worn, they tended to rot.

Our summer uniform was quite different and for juniors consisted of check cotton dresses with short sleeves, reaching to a 'decent' length below the knee. These were home-made

and could be either in school blue or in house colours; in practice most people had at least one of each. Seniors wore navy-and-white-striped dresses, and sixth-formers wore dresses with stripes of their relevant house colours. In the summer most schools changed from gymslips and skirts to dresses. Gingham was popular, usually in checks and in blue, red or green to reflect school and house colours – one school even managed 'a kind of subtle check of pinks and blues'. The next most common were striped dress, again of relevant colours. At one school the only concession to the arrival of summer was the shedding of ties.

In the summer term our berets were replaced, as elsewhere, by very unpopular boaters; expensive to buy, stiff and uncomfortable to wear, and sticky if the wearer was caught in a shower. Some people used to keep a plastic bag handy to put over them as they smelt unpleasant when wet. Girls with plastic bags on their heads looked less than smart, in fact they looked ridiculous, but they were obeying rules and wearing hats in public at all times. In the summer of 1963 boaters were suddenly popular (with those who weren't forced to wear them), probably due to the popularity of the 1920s-style pop group the Temperance Seven. That year those boaters belonging to school-leavers could be sold rather than thrown into the moat, as had come to be the tradition. Other types of summer hat were a Panama hat with hat band.

There was little scope for innovations or improvements that you could make to school wear, although nearly everybody hitched up the skirts and made them stand out with at least one net petticoat underneath. Petticoats were made up of several layers of net and came in horribly bright colours. To achieve the maximum effect, one hauled the lot up until the petticoats stuck out like a sunshade, then turned the waistbands over several times, which made even the slimmest wearer look like a bolster and the thickset like a mattress. Not only did these monstrosities prick the thighs and scratch their way round the back of the knees, causing rashes as they did so, they also developed minds of their own. They would shoot up at the front like a crinoline when one sat down – particularly awkward in a church pew. When in need of a wash, the things went limp and flopped in a most unhelpful manner, being coaxed back to life again only by several applications of sugar water. After this they perked up, stuck to anything they made contact with and resumed their scratching of bare young flesh and constructing little holes in one's stockings. A pair of stockings might cost 4/6d, 5/11d or even as much as 6/6d and so, apart from looking scruffy, having to replace them took quite a chunk out of our already meagre finances.

In addition to all this finery, parents had to pay out for games kits; to call this sportswear would be flattering it. This consisted of yellow aertex shirts, of the kind that are now called polo shirts, and grey pleated shorts. For gym (as opposed to playing a sport) and dance classes we were down to shirts and navy knickers. The obligatory vests were to be taken off before and replaced after a games class in order to absorb the sweat. This was done as an alternative to showering, seeing as the school had none. In the second year we had to make what were known as dance tunics to wear for gym and dance classes. These were really basic affairs (they needed to be with our limited skills as needlewomen), mid-thigh length with short, cap sleeves and elastic where the waist was supposed to be. There was a choice of colours: china blue, crimson, Lincoln green and a sickly salmon pink.

For hockey we were expected to provide a stick (ready bound in adhesive tape to protect the wood), very thick grey socks and rubber-soled lace-up boots. It was possible to buy second-hand hockey kit or even borrow it for a class, but nobody did. Tennis gear was much more popular and we vied with each other as to what brand of racquet (and press) we had, although the most popular item of all our uniform was our tennis shoes. One of the most prestigious was Dunlop Green Flash, with its satisfyingly thick and spongy sole. Many of us attempted to keep our tennis shoes on during the day, but the rule about reverting to our indoor shoes was strictly enforced. Our feet had to be allowed to breathe so we would be saved from the foot rot, which might otherwise have been contracted by remaining in sweaty sports shoes.

In regard to hair-dos to go with all this fashionable gear, in theory hair was expected to be short enough to be kept off the collar, or tied neatly back. School photos from the period, however, show that these expectations weren't always met. There is evidence of perms: some tightly curled to the head, others growing out and tatty, but both showing signs of frizz. Although tidy, ponytails, tightly confined by an elastic band, were frowned upon by hair-care experts who claimed that this continued pulling of the hair in one direction might cause it to split, and eventually even recede. The history mistress would tell us that we looked like little horses with our pony tails. Hardly an original observation, but she was pleased with it and repeated it quite frequently.

The beehive, that most unhealthy and usually unflatter-ing of hairstyles, arrived in 1958 and lasted as high fashion until 1962; with adaptations it limped on into the middle of the decade. The style, which was more like a bird's nest, required constant attention by way of backcombing and lacquering into place – the hair being rarely, if ever, given a good brushing between the constructing of hives. Any hair that was bold enough to attempt to stray was brutally poked back into its proper place with the end of a tail comb, and immediately re-lacquered. If caught in a shower of rain, the beehives became a sticky mess on the top of the owner's head. So important was the role of hair lacquer that special shampoos were introduced to combat build-up on the hair. School cloakrooms were packed with girls wedged in elbow to elbow, all bobbing up and down in an attempt to see in the mirror, spraying lacquer into each other's faces and all over the mirror, and trying to persuade their friends to back-comb that elusive wad which stubbornly remained out of reach of their aching arms.

Hair colourants were cheap and easy to use. They varied in strength from the colouring shampoo ('Hint of a Tint'), which disappeared with the next wash, through to semi-permanents, which withstood several washings and could be put up with if it turned out to be disappointing. The permanents were the hard stuff of the hair-colour world and you needed to treat these with respect! One that went wrong once resulted in a classmate's gorgeous raven-black hair being ruined by a marmalade-coloured wing at the front, which took the rest of the school year and the following holidays to grow out. Another casualty was a fair-haired fourth-former who intended to go blonde but ended up a nauseous shade of green. This experience didn't put her off hair colorants as she left the following summer and went to the local tech to study hairdressing, perhaps in order to learn how to avoid making the same mistake again.

General rules in all schools stated 'No jewellery allowed', 'Schoolgirls are not expected to have pierced ears' and 'Long hair had to be tied back at all times'. Trousers were never worn by either girls or teachers. At one or two schools, girls wore their own choice of clothes in the sixth form, something which was introduced when our own year was in the sixth.

Anyone who went to more than one school, and this wasn't uncommon when parents were in the armed forces or any other occupation that involved moving round the country, needed a complete new uniform for each one, even though it might be worn for only a year or two.

Four

Be True to Your School, The Beach Boys, 1963

Of course we all shuffled into the hall for assembly every morning, heard prayers, sang a hymn, listened with half an ear to any notices which were given out and shuffled out again to the accompaniment of orders not to slouch and to pull our cardigan sleeves down to cover our forearms – but that was the total extent of corporate involvement as far as we were concerned.

The first to fourth forms were subject to a classroom inspection each week. Marks out of ten were awarded for flowers and for desk tidiness, and out of five for 'overall general impression'. Offenders, the contents of whose desks were left in a mess, were shamed by having the desk lids left open for all to see. At the end of each term the form with the greatest number of marks were given an award, usually a vase.

There was no school hymn or any other type of song at our school, and if there had been it's doubtful whether it would have been appreciated. Neither did we have a school magazine or any sort of archive. Lord Williams's Grammar School (LWGS), on the other hand, could boast a bilingual school hymn *Jesu Redemptor Omnium* (*Jesu Redeemer of us all*), to be sung in Latin and English. There, as befitted a foundation dating back to the mid-sixteenth century, were the full range of celebrations: founder's day, old boys versus school match and so on. The first magazine at LWGS was called the *Mercury*, which later changed to *The Tamensian*. The hardcopy version had a drawing of Lord Williams pointing to the crest with *a tous venants* underneath – *The Tamensian* is now online complete with its public school *Salvete* and *Valete* entries.

School hymns and songs are either memorable or easily forgotten. Of course, like ours, some schools didn't have one in the first place. Tonbridge had both a hymn, *Now Thank we all our God*, and 'a school song which was straight out of Enid Blyton'! The chorus was something to the effect:

School on the hilltop keep our devotion, True amid all life's fears, May our tradition of courage and honour grow, grow, with the passing years.

At Plymouth High School for Girls the song was the same as the motto, *Non scholae sed vitae discimus*. 'This was tough on those who didn't know Latin, but only the lowest group didn't do Latin. You had to have O level Latin then to read an arts subject at university, and as science was not encouraged at school, Latin was a *sine qua non*.' The song was specially written for the school. Cheney School's was *Our Father by whose Servants our House was Built of Old* and South

Shields Grammar School girls started the day with *Morning has Broken*, soon to be turned into a hit by Cat Stevens and said to be useful for getting sleepy offspring out of bed. At Tollington School they sang their allegiance to *The Dear Old Green and Gold*. The one at Cirencester Grammar School was *He who would Valiant be,* and at Queen Elizabeth's, *We Build our School on Thee, Oh Lord.* Ilkley's *Once More to Part* was written by a former teacher. Eccles adopted *I Vow to thee my Country* and County High School, Wellingborough had two specially composed Christmas carols; 'No School hymn as such. We always sang *Lord Dismiss us with Thy Blessing* at the end of the school year.'

Southgate County Grammar School had a school song, *Ad Lucem*, with the 'memorable' chorus:

Onward, unswerving into the fight;
Seeking no rest till the goal's in sight;
'Tis life's golden way.
So here's to the task of setting self right.

Chichester's High School for Girls' school song was the rousing *Sussex by the Sea*, the words being a poem by Rudyard Kipling. At Ursuline High School, Ilford, 'there was one but I can't remember a thing about it'. As for Fairford, Barnstaple and Andover: 'I can't remember if we had a school hymn or song at any of the schools.' Similarly, there was said to be none at Walthamstow.

Our school had a motto that could be seen stitched in gold on the blazer pocket. It read *'Palma non sine pulvere'* ('No Palms without Dust'). It is derived from Horace's *First Epistle*, in which he asks *'sit condicio dulcis sine pulvere palmae?'* – in other words, anything worth having is worth working for. Our motto was already in use by the Friend's

School of Baltimore, a Quaker school founded in 1784. The words surrounded a picture of the House, crenulations and all, while our male counterparts at Lord Bill's were told '*Sic itur ad astra*' ('You shall go to the stars' – reach for the stars, even – from Virgil's *Aeneid*, Book IX). The pupils of Tonbridge Girls' Grammar School, founded in 1905, were told to possess 'Courage and Honour'; while the motto of Plymouth High School for Girls sounds like one of the most sensible mottos of all: '*Non scholae sed vitae discimus*' ('For life not school we learn'). In reality, it was quite the other way round. Regarding Chichester High School's motto, an alumna admitted: 'Can't remember. Not the one on the present website, I'm sure.'

We held no founder's day celebrations at our school, probably because the school had no founder to honour. Prize days were highly forgettable. They were held in November in the gym-cum-art room where most (but not quite all) the powder paint had been scraped off the parquet flooring. Prizes were awarded principally for obtaining Grade 1 in O level subjects and for A level passes. In addition, there were one or two unique ones, such as the head girl's prize. A glance at the photographs taken by the local press reveals some rather surprising choices of prize – some of the favourites being geography and cookery books. The whole school was required to attend and a successful academic, usually female – of whom few if any of us had heard – was invited to present the prizes. One exception was in 1961 when a pupil who had recently won a prize in a *Daily Mail* competition about the EEC addressed the gathering. After the handing over of the prize books and the guest speaker's talk Miss D. would deliver a homily of her own, by which time the younger members of her audience had been reduced to a soporific state.

There were no formal sports days as such, let alone those of the type held by the girls of the city grammar school a few miles down the road. They played all sorts of sports and games on their sports day, including cricket, netball, tennis and hockey, and even croquet, slow bicycle and a flower-pot race. No activities were arranged outside hours for the general student body either, only sports matches against other schools taking place at the weekends. Teams from school entered local sports tournaments and in 1956 the first netball VII reached the finals of the county tournament, in which it drew but lost the cup on goal average. Inter-house tennis, netball and hockey matches were apparently 'eagerly awaited' by all in the early 1950s, but by the end of the decade only the contenders showed much interest in them. The hockey cup was presented by the parent-teacher association and the tennis shield was given by the old girls' association. In the summer term there was a doubles tennis tournament for a cup, which had been presented by a parent.

Some schools had separate speech days, sports days and founder's days, while at others they were a combined occasion. Apart from us, nearly every school had at least two of the three red-letter days, with varying degrees of importance attached to each, as the following testaments show:

Sports day was very important; there was also school play, and speech day – when they had excellent famous speakers.

We had prize days and sports days. I don't think parents were invited. One special occasion was the official school opening ceremony, held in the hall of the Poly next door. Ruth Spooner gave a speech [daughter of the spoonerism man].

Founder's day, Sports day: all of those annually, plus a school fete one year …

There were prize days. I won class prizes at both of them I think. I assume there were Sports Days but can't remember them specifically.

Founder's Day doubled up as the prize day, held each autumn in the Guildhall. Dull speeches by dull Aldermen and Alderwomen telling us to work hard. Sports day was held at the Brickfields sports track in Devonport. Smaller events such as the Public Speaking Competition were held in the school hall.

These festivities sound the most fun:

Speech Day was held at the local baths (the pool was covered of course!) and parents were invited. Founder's Day was held in the parish church and the Mayor usually attended. Sports Day was held on our own fields and teachers also took part. The annual male versus female teachers netball match was always popular.

Another school held two prize days, one for lower school and one for upper school, but there was no sports day as all sports were inter-house. One school was quite different in that it held a prize night.

Every year in the early to mid-1950s our school would hold a birthday fete – originally held in June, it later moved to July because of the Oxford Local Examinations the previous month. This fete consisted of sideshows, various stalls and competitions. Teas and other refreshments were served by the senior girls, while the sideshows and competitions were the responsibility of the fifth form, and the junior ones for the stalls. A local celebrity came along to open the event, usually someone connected with the school or a parent. In the mid-1950s the local press covered the 'entertainment', where a fete was held in our 'extensive grounds'. It was opened by an aristocratic lady who cheerfully admitted in her opening speech that she'd not had much to do with girls' schools as she had three boys. Fortunately, she'd had plenty of experience in opening events. The fete was organised by the girls themselves and attractions included such delights as: bowling, electric wire, trade names, find the donkey's tail, hidden lambs, balls in the bucket, cork pinning, test your smell, guessing the number of peas, weight of the cake, weight of groceries and a bran tub. There were stalls selling groceries, vegetables and needlework made by the pupils. Needless to say, refreshments were also available.

That year a concert of songs and music on the piano and recorder was also held in the school hall. The singing was said to be pleasant but 'there was not enough variety in tone and the intonation in the harmony was often poor'. In the evening a play was put on, of which critics were somewhat harsh of the youthful efforts:

> … the choice of which did not suit an all-girls' school, in so much as the plot of *She Stoops to Conquer* depends a lot on the strength of the male parts … Throughout the play the weakness was that the cast seemed in a hurry to get it over with and by speaking too quickly, and without clarity, lines were lost to the audience.

Fundraising fetes to raise the money to pay for a swimming pool followed at the end of the 1950s. These took the usual pattern of stalls, games, a raffle and refreshments. After a fete was over, everyone (including parents who were planning to take their offspring home by car) would be coerced into going round picking up litter and putting it into a series of bins in the grounds. Nobody was allowed to leave until everywhere was pristine. One year this had a strange sequel for, when we arrived the following morning, the lawns looked much worse than they had done before the litter collection had even started. Each and every one of the bins was surrounded by a circle of paper cake cups, apple cores, cartons and, above all, ice-cream wrappers. As we watched we noticed a squirrel licking the last vestiges of ice cream off some paper, a look of dreamy ecstasy on its face.

Examples of pupils' work adorned the walls of all the classrooms and once one of the shortest dramatic productions on record took place 'for today only' in Room Z. This was the 'rude mechanicals' play from *A Midsummer Night's Dream* and in this Auntie Dottie showed genius. Apart from its admirable brevity, which allowed little scope for boredom to run riot among members of the audience, the roles were ideal for our limited talents. The main players, the classical lovers Pyramus and Thisbe, gave great scope for hamming it up while the rest of the workmen could be played with rustic phlegm, which came naturally to many of the residents of our part of the world. It would be satisfying to relate how, after the criticism of their predecessors' performance in *She Stoops to Conquer*, this *Dream* cast received rave reviews and moved on to the West End, but alas, this was not the case.

Much more professional was the Shakespearian cross-dressing, which had been a feature of drama at the boys' school for several years previously. An introduction to the work of the bard was extended to us Shakespeare virgins by way of, firstly, *Twelfth Night* and, later, *The Taming of the Shrew* – both presented by the grammar school boys. *Twelfth Night* was produced out in the open in the school grounds in front of a small audience who sat very close to the actors in true Tudor fashion; the *Shrew* took place in the shelter of the town hall. It was fascinating for those of us who knew them in their blazers and grey flannels to see the boys transformed, the older ones into demigods in richly coloured doublet and hose. The younger boys were returning to the ancient tradition of boys taking female roles before actresses eventually became 'respectable', so our young friends appeared in floor-length dresses, wigs and rouge without the slightest sign of self-consciousness. These dramatic performances did bear fruit for one youthful actor who went from being Maria in *Twelfth Night* to Captain Birdseye in the fish-finger television commercials.

In the autumn term of 1961, the boys abandoned their Shakespearian tradition of casting junior boys in girls' parts and took the radical step of importing talent from our school. Referring to their previous practice, *The Tamensian* commented, 'the School apparently succumbed to the modern theory that female parts are best played by females. Whether this departure indicated mounting virility or declining versatility was uncertain'. The play was *Cerano de Bergerac* and the venue the hall of the newly opened comprehensive school, which was destined to merge with Lord Williams's when the comprehensive system was adopted in the county. The girls who 'risked joining the cast' included five members of our own year. 'That said,' concludes The *Tamensian*, 'the production was deemed excellent.' Not surprisingly, co-ed schools had the advantage of being able to offer a wider range of plays, which were more convincing with both sexes taking the appropriate roles.

The amount and content of dramatic productions varied from school to school. Nothing at all in that line was done at one, at another there were only 'infrequent dramatics', while at a third the response 'Not me, but some did' implies that this was not a particularly high-ranking activity. One year *Jane Eyre* was produced in the form of a play and elsewhere the girls put on 'plays (in French one year); some kind of mixed entertainment one year'. Every year at another school there was a school play held in the naval theatre at Devonport for parents and pupils, and a house drama festival. Shakespearian productions were among the most common, as well as Gilbert & Sullivan. Another all-girls school hosted the sixth-form play, as well as concerts and plays with the local boys' school, but the most unusual events were the public-speaking contests.

> *Don't know much about history,*
> *Don't know much biology,*
> *Don't know much about a science book,*
> *Don't know much about the French I took …*
> *Wonderful World*, Sam Cooke, 1960

In our day there were about a dozen teachers – mostly full time – but no male teachers. Indeed, the only men on the premises were employed to deal with maintenance; one was quite young (although he didn't seem so to us), the other a dear little gnome of a man. The headmistress had been in post since the school had opened. Miss D., sometimes referred to as Daisy, had her own flat in the extension to the main house and was in charge of senior maths. Earlier descriptions of her mention her kindness and good humour towards her pupils, but by our time she seldom smiled and was looked on as being unapproachable. She had problems with her spine and her lack of bonhomie would have been due to her increasing disability, but of course as selfish teenagers we were quite unaware of this.

Some of the subjects on the curriculum, notably English, French, maths and geography, were compulsory for the whole five years, whether or not the O level examination was taken. We were divided into two groups according to our ability. There were two teachers of maths: Miss W., the only-too-easy-to-bully subject teacher, and, at the other end of the social scale, the headmistress herself; from the sublime to the ridiculous. Maths, which had sounded so grown up before we graduated from mere arithmetic, soon proved to be a source of incomprehension for several of us. We were never able to get to grips with geometry despite the patient teacher's willingness to go over it time and time again, to the extent of drawing in angles, figures etc. with different coloured chalk. All was fine while the examples were still on display, but the minute that they were wiped off minds went just as blank as the board.

By the end of four years' copying, avoiding and guessing (which still led to a distressing number of D and E grades in our maths exercise books) at least we could tell a triangle from a square. Algebra was even worse, if that was possible, for anyone unable to do more than remove the brackets and wonder what they were doing there in the first place. As we were all forced to carry on with maths, during the fifth year the situation became even more stressful as we were abandoned by Miss W. and handed over to the head for the unspeakable torture of double maths in the afternoon, something which cast a black cloud over the preceding morning. On several occasions, one of us got herself into such a state of nerves that she was sick and had to go and lie down. Daisy was unexpectedly lenient with those of us who were non-starters in the mathematical stakes and very kindly ignored us, concentrating instead on the handful who volunteered answers.

Miss S., or 'Auntie Dottie' as she was affectionately called, was described in the 1955 education report as a 'young

London graduate in post since 1952'. By the time that we arrived she'd become the senior English mistress and in charge of the third form. Before that she had been helped out by the craft mistress, but we had some lessons with the second French teacher when we were in the second year. The report laments the fact that the girls' 'Private reading not of the same quality as that read in class', but doesn't say how they'd got hold of that fact. Auntie Dottie could well have been a chalk thrower in her younger days and, if she'd been teaching at a boys' school, probably not averse to a quick slap or application of the ruler. As it was, she kept order because she was quick-witted and known to be fair. She therefore found a place in our affections as well as commanding our respect. English classes brought all of us together, culminating in the O level English language and English literature examinations, which were taken by everybody.

Miss E., the sole geography mistress, was in charge of the fourth years. Geography was a strong subject at all levels throughout the school, as the examination results show. She was described in the report as a 'Well-qualified and experienced specialist', with 'High standards set at all times' so that her 'prestige with the pupils is such that these standards are realised', which may account for the fact that she never had a nickname, flattering or otherwise. The inspectors who compiled the 1955 report found it unfortunate that Miss E.'s room was deficient, in that it was not possible for the room to be made dark enough for an episcope (a type of projector) to be used properly. It went on to say that, 'This mistress proposes to give further rein to individual initiative and discrimination'. As far as we were concerned at the time, Miss E. was best known for her commands to 'Go and wash that stuff off your finger nails', which involved tripping off to the lab to ask to 'borrow' some acetone. She also supervised our attempts at debating during the lunch hour with a poker face, coping with topics such as 'Would you prefer to live in the town or the country?' (result: town), and the very audacious 'Do you think that girls should still be virgins on their wedding day?' (a hypocritical yes to this). There were no field trips or visits to relevant sites in preparation for O levels at our school, although pupils from most of the other schools were taken somewhere.

French was taught in sets, with the subject compulsory at some level throughout the first five years. French, like geography, was said to be 'particularly well taught', even though there was only one teacher for each of these subjects in 1955. That was Miss W., the deputy head, also known as 'The Worthy Bird'. Pronunciation was said to be carefully taught and 'by dint of plentiful chorus work', as she would make sure that everyone spoke in her classes. The deputy head was, by default, the senior French mistress, the other French teacher, who also taught some English, taught up to O level. This was 'Aggie' (so called because the initials of her first names were A.A.G.), who was also form mistress for the second years. She went off on maternity leave before we left the school. This came as a considerable shock to all of us as all the teachers seemed as old as God, if not older, and in any case they were dowdily dressed and wore little or no make-up – apart from the history teacher's rouge. An earlier policy had been for second year girls to be 'twinned' with a French family for exchange visits during the school holidays. Where successful, these contacts lasted well beyond schooldays and into adult life. French was another new undertaking (there was no Latin until the second year), and it was the sort of subject you either take to or you don't. Until we could understand French as used by the French (as opposed to passages from a textbook, a very different proposition), our perception of the language and people was vague and indifferent. French classes were not too taxing and, therefore, were to be tolerated; the homework a necessary evil. At our most enthusiastic we saw it as little more than a useful O level subject.

In the third year it became fashionable to have penfriends; the more exotic the better. It was intriguing to think of one's own letter jetting off to a country that one had hardly heard of and which had to be looked up in an atlas. These friendships seldom lasted beyond the first couple of letters, largely due to language problems, the expense of buying stamps and airmail stationery, and the sheer effort of having to go into the post office to have letters weighed. However, if we were lucky we might find a correspondent who would send all sorts of cards and photos of current French stars of screen and recording studio, such as Jacques Brel, Roger Vadim, Sasha Distel and, of course, Bardot. Then, in the fourth year, we might find a penfriend who would be capable of exchanging gossip, fashion news, scandal and opinions. This might lead to the arrival of French teenage magazines and pop records. This was a revelation! From the magazines we quickly discovered that teenagers across the Channel were very similar to us and that French was in fact a modern language that could be used to talk about boyfriends and pop stars and make-up, not just describe schoolrooms and grammar and strange Gallic customs. With such riveting material to work on, our colloquial French improved by leaps and bounds and to practise our pronunciation we would repeat the song lyrics like parrots, sometimes getting the meaning completely wrong.

The fact that our studies of modern languages were confined to French put pupils at a great disadvantage if they wanted to study the subject at university, and only two of the other schools in this book were in this situation. Unlike the majority, we weren't able to take German (except for the Scouse incomer who was once allowed to do so as she was almost at O level standard when she arrived). At one school it was considered: 'If you did Latin, you couldn't do German as well. German results poor, as those who were bad at English and French in the first form were relegated to the German class in the second form.' Far more cosmopolitan was the school that offered Spanish as an optional extra O level in the lower sixth, another school where 'a smattering of Russian' was available and a third school where girls were taught Italian.

Mrs P., the science mistress, had no form to look after. Her nickname was 'Flora' and her popularity was earned by her relaxed attitude and dry sense of humour. The 1955 report has several criticisms to make of science at our school, none of which reflects badly on the teaching. There was some 'Instability of staffing' as well as 'Insufficient teaching space in the laboratory', resulting in 'Possible risks from overcrowding'. Biology was the strongest subject, it said, with 'A few girls able to take Human Biology', while general science at O level was taken by the first-form mistress, Miss W., who does her best to 'grapple with the problems involved in laboratory work, some of which are unfamiliar to her', which doesn't sound all that encouraging.

Flora turned her hand to all of the science subjects available throughout the school. General science consisted of physics, chemistry and biology. Also, 'science' was optional as separate O levels in chemistry and physics. The lab had rather scruffy benches carved with various names, covered with the usual Bunsen burners, pipettes and jars. Among Flora's little idiosyncrasies were grass snakes stored in the fridge and a jar of leeches, which stood on the window sill. If a girl put her hand down on some fragments of broken glass, the leeches, or one of them, leapt into action. A volunteer was fastened

on to the cut and left to do its business. The sensation was of an initial sharp pricking when it made its Y-shaped incision, and then a not-unpleasant tickling. Any clean cuts, which might otherwise have benefited from a stitch or two, were promptly sealed in Bunsen burner flame and that was the end of it. By popular demand, end-of-term treats in the lab were watching blobs of mercury roll around on the bench top and, even more spectacularly, the spontaneous combustion of a chunk of phosphorous when exposed to the air.

The science subjects are difficult to define, ranging as they do from maths to general science. The latter could be taken at all the grammar schools either as a combined subject, individually as the 'big three' (biology, chemistry and physics) or, as for one set of girls, restricted to biology and chemistry. General science to O level, then biology, physics and chemistry to A level, was typical. At another school all three could be done to O level:

> … although I gave up both Physics and Chemistry altogether at the tender age of 12. Sciences were not encouraged, and for A-level you could only do these combinations: Biology and Art or Physics and Chemistry. Hence those who wanted to read sciences at university had to work on Biology A-level by themselves at home.

In the sixth form at another school: 'these were sub-divided into all sorts of options, especially Maths which was offered in four different varieties, I think! The school was very strong in science, and had as many girls doing maths and physics at "A"-level as it did English and History.' Six schools offered the usual three, as did another with the addition of zoology and botany. The most scientifically minded of all the schools surveyed in this book was in a position to teach chemistry, physics, biology and general science at O level, and chemistry, physics, biology, zoology and botany at A level.

In 1955 a pre-nursing course was still running at our school, but had been removed from the curriculum by the time our year arrived. Human biology & hygiene could be taken at O level and, though it was considered by some to be of a lower status than one of the 'pure' sciences, the lessons were interesting and the pass rate high. They were taken by the games mistress, using her knowledge of anatomy and physiology. Quite a few people in the lower sixth chose to add human biology & hygiene to their first set of O levels, but the subject was not available at A level. We could choose whether or not to take other subjects at O level, the decision being a joint one between the pupil and the teacher, although it depended largely on the mock O level results. Other subjects had to be dropped in the run-up to O levels, and it was also decided whether one was in the upper or lower fifth; taking French and Latin meant no cookery or needlework.

'Bessie', the Latin mistress who was in charge of the upper fifth, had a London degree in classics as well as a splendid Roman nose, which caused one or two speculations as to whether this had been what prompted her to read the subject in the first place. She had taught mainly in private schools before she was appointed in 1955. The 1955 education report commented that there was 'vigorous classroom teaching' but 'more careful attention needs to be given to correct pronunciation from the very beginning'. Each year about half the year's intake started Latin in the second year, and those who did so were 'selected mainly on ability in English and French'. We were allowed to give up Latin in fourth form and do domestic science in its place, but nobody in our year did so. Bessie was later awarded the British Empire Medal and became head teacher of the comprehensive school that succeeded our own. Latin wasn't always an easy option, in fact there were tears towards the end of the first term with requests to drop the subject. Bessie was very patient and went through all our problems and queries one by one until we cheered up and agreed to go on. In 1960, Latin was dropped by Oxford as a classical language (one of which was compulsory for entry).

The end-of-term treats consisted of doing very basic crosswords and singing *Ardet Roma* (the equivalent of *London's Burning*), and *Quem Pastores* if it was the end of the autumn term. There are quite a few things which are remembered from Latin classes: the verb 'to be' never takes an object and the fact that there seemed to be nearly as many exceptions as examples when learning a declension, but what stands out as if it were yesterday is the rhyme told to us in the first term in an attempt to show that Latin can be fun. It went:

Caesar adsum iam forte (Caesar had some jam for tea)
Pompey ad erat (Pompey had a rat)
Caesar sic in omnibus (Caesar sick in omnibus)
Pompey in is at (Pompey in his hat)

Also imprinted on the brain forever is an early piece for translation from Latin concerning the *tres parvi porci* and their nemesis, the Big Bad Wolf. We were spared the harrowing details of the demise of Pigs One and Two and taken to the culmination when *lupus flabat et flabat sed frustra,* but despite all the huffing and puffing was unable to blow down the third little piggy's brick dwelling. This was all deeply satisfying for a 12-year-old for its portrayal of evil getting its comeuppance. Latin was not something that was commonly taken at A level; only one member of our year obtained a pass in the subject. Latin was offered at all the other schools researched, with the addition of varying amounts of Ancient Greek at five of them

The history mistress, of whom there was only the one, was a first-class honours graduate of Sheffield University, and she too had been there since the school opened. Mrs A. was a bird-like creature with an eternally grown-out perm and bright splodges of rouge on her cheeks. She was normally dressed in a grey suit and wore shoes with thick high heels (open-toed in the summer) of the type favoured by Minnie Mouse, and Princess Margaret too, come to think of it. For some reason she was known to us as Ariadne. According to the memories of one old girl, in the late 1940s and early '50s Mrs A. would take pupils on extra-curricular field trips at the weekend in her own car, visiting local historical sites such as Roman villas. In 1955 it was said of history that there was 'Too heavy an emphasis on the last 150 years', there was a reliance on the 'use of radio programmes' and in the lower forms a good deal of 'sheer copying', but on the other hand there was a 'Good use of local history and current affairs' so that history was 'clearly a subject which is enjoyed by many'.

Our own introduction to history at grammar-school level started with *How Things Began*, a radio programme which necessitated our drawing dinosaurs of unspecified type with a background of swamps and tree ferns. The broadcast was, in fact, more relevant to biology and zoology than to history proper, although quite entertaining and informative in its own right. History classes went on to include tales about the school's resident and visiting ghosts, and a few anecdotes about historic personalities. Other favourite topics were etiquette and dress codes, notably when to wear gloves and of what colour, material and length. Last and usually least were the lists of monarchs and dates, which were compulsory learning at that period. Any question that required candidates to discuss a topic would have been beyond most people's experience. If Ariadne considered that a pupil hadn't been working as hard as she might have done immediately before taking mocks, she deliberately marked her paper down so that she failed by half a mark. As this was an optional O level, some retaliated by dropping the subject altogether.

Art was the province of the inimitable Mrs H., who sported a series of short-sleeved T-shirts of varying hues under a green corduroy pinafore dress and who, like us, wore ankle socks (but coloured ones) and sandals. Whether they were good for art or not, no one was sure. One of most people's enduring memories of their time at our school must be sitting out on the grass across from the island sketching the blossom in pastels on a warm spring day. There were some spectacular autumn colours as well, but it was generally too cold and damp to be able to spend much time sitting around by then. Art could be given up in the fifth form and often was by those who needed more 'serious' subjects in order to get into university. However, it was a popular additional O level taken by pupils in the lower sixth.

Mrs H. was married to an eminent historian at the University of Oxford and lived in the manor house in the nearby village. One summer afternoon the fifth-form art class (not ours, unfortunately) was invited to tea there. As they arrived Mrs H. was called to the phone, so they were told to go out into the garden where they got into conversation with a rather dishevelled middle-aged man who was busily digging over the flower beds. Mrs H. reappeared and enquired if they'd met her husband William, to which they replied no, but that they'd been talking to the gardener. 'That,' said Mrs H., '*is* William!' In first year only we had one-hour lessons in italic handwriting from Mrs H. on Monday afternoons. Some of us discarded it the minute the lesson was over, but one or two adopted it and developed their writing into something approaching calligraphy.

Miss B., an elegant dark-haired lady with a chignon, was in charge of domestic science and was also the form mistress of the lower fifth. Despite this fact, she remained something of an unknown quantity and was spoken of with respect; indeed, she had no nickname and nobody seemed to know her first name. Domestic science (more usually called DS), that is needlework and cookery, formalised some activities which we'd dabbled with since we were children and introduced us to others, such as nutrition. The 1955 education report comments unfavourably on the DS room (but not on the teaching itself), saying that two of the cookers were very small, the hot water supply inadequate, the room very overcrowded and the allowance for materials quite inadequate for both cookery and needlework, all of which resulted in the fact that 'unsuitable patterns as well as materials have been purchased by the examination candidates themselves'.

Both needlework and cookery were compulsory in the junior forms and later taken as separate O levels. On one occasion the domestic science room had to be evacuated while an O level exam was actually in progress, when a tray of meringues rose, stuck on the roof of the oven and created clouds of black smoke. Even though our DS facilities were crowded and inadequate, they were preferable to classes at another girls' grammar school where girls had to learn 'housewifery' and pupils had instruction in cutting-edge skills such as how to black-lead a grate and scrub a table. Cookery at another didn't sound like much fun: 'Cookery aprons were white cotton, made by pupils when they were in the second form to wear in the third form for cookery. (I could write a whole essay on the horrors of cookery.)'

The music mistresses changed when we were at the school. The first, Miss P., is mentioned in the education report as being a part-time mistress, a graduate of the Guildhall School of Music, who had just started in 1955 when the inspectors arrived. She held private violin lessons and a recorder class, and had eight private piano pupils at the school. The violins were on loan from the educational authority at half a crown a term, but pupils had to buy their own recorders. Some gramophone records were owned by the school and those in the county library could be borrowed. One drawback was that the gramophone 'cannot be adapted for use with long-playing records'.

During our first few terms the main thing that we did in music periods was rehearse the assembly hymns for the week to come. Among our favourites were those with rousing tunes, such as *Onward Christian Soldiers* and *The Battle Hymn of the Republic*, as well as a few which we'd learnt during our recently started Sunday-morning visits to church, prior to being confirmed. These included *O, Jesus, I Have Promised* and *Dear Lord and Father of Mankind*. We progressed to learning about the composition of music and writing it down in our books, which were ready printed with staves. All we had to do was fill in the clefs and place the notes in their correct positions, something which eluded me completely. A few girls took lessons on the violin or oboe and their faltering efforts were to be heard throughout the building in the afternoon, the screeches of the violin and melancholy pipe of the oboe. Music was an optional O level, which was only chosen by a couple of people.

Our music classes were very basic compared with most of our counterparts in grammar schools around the country. Nearly all of the other schools had a least one orchestra and hosted concerts on a regular basis. At one there were several orchestras: 'we also prepared something musical for speech day. I seem to remember singing chunks of the *Magic Flute*.

Because the school drew from a very wide catchment area, after-school activities were limited, and often only those who lived close participated.' One school hosted a music festival in the school hall, although admission was for pupils only; another held annual Christmas carol services; and at a third there were regular dramatic and musical productions or recitals. Among those staged elsewhere were: '*Amahl and the Night Visitors* (a Menotti opera), *Trial by Jury* (G&S) with the local boys' school. Musical activities increased enormously when a new young music teacher appeared when I was about fifteen.' One reply regarding musical performances was as follows: 'There must have been but don't remember any! Just Jimmy Savile coming to DJ our leavers' dance!'

One of the co-ed schools was exceptionally fortunate in having one of the country's leading composers as music master from 1959 to 1962. He wrote many works for the school choir and orchestra. The school took part in the Bath Festival in 1962 when Yehudi Menuhin played a composition by one of the pupils. An old girl particularly remembers *St John Passion*, *St Matthew Passion* and *Noye's Fludde* at carol and founder's day, as well as at numerous other concerts, churches and festivals. At another school the carol service was a huge event and another even held theirs in the local cathedral.

Mrs R. was the mistress in charge of physical education who also taught O level human biology & hygiene. She had no form responsibilities and no nickname, although the fact that her daughter's name was Imogen rather impressed us. As with other subjects, the 1955 education report was critical of the school's facilities but not of the teacher; the gym had:

> ... inferior accommodation as no fixed apparatus, only
> 22 girls can play hockey at one time [in the event, this was

about 20 more than wanted to play and the most pressing
need was for changing rooms and showers]. At present,
the girls have to remain for the rest of the day in the same
clothes in which they have taken vigorous exercise, a most
undesirable practice.

Most of the class avoided the perils of 'vigorous exercise'
by doggedly avoiding it whenever possible. The report
concludes that the school was most lucky to have Mrs R.,
under whom 'the girls work with enjoyment and zest', but
that of course was in 1955. In theory, at least, games were
compulsory throughout the school. Initially, there was only
Mrs R., who took everything from dancing and gym to
hockey, tennis and netball. Two other teachers arrived during
our time at the school and took us for games with markedly
less success.

Tennis was generally very popular throughout the school
and there was always fierce competition to use the courts
in the dinner hour. This was achieved by being the first to
arrive there – possession being nine-tenths of the law – after
lunch had been gobbled down. Jen was our usual choice as
representative, for not only was she a swift eater but she
was also quick on her feet. As for netball, we had all played
with boys as well as girls at primary school. Some had experience of nuns being quite skilled at the game, kilting up their
heavy skirts and running and jumping with the best of us.
Netball was popular in the winter and was played not only
during games sessions but also informally with shooting and
defence sessions every dinner hour. After the initial novelty
had worn off, somewhere around the first fortnight of our
first term, hockey was by and large loathed and avoided if
at all possible. Similarly, enforced 'running', in gold shirt and
navy knickers, was violently objected to and even boycotted.

Dancing, heavily influenced by the then trendy school of method acting, took place only in the first form and was tolerated as being amusing – we made fools of ourselves by turning into trees and waves. Later, when in the fifth form, we were invited to learn ballroom dancing during periods timetabled for gym; there were very few enthusiasts, although Latin American dances were found to be quite fun. Even though we were very keen jivers, rock 'n' rollers and twisters, more sedate dancing was considered very passé. Gym lessons were not generally enjoyed, either. They failed to live up to the picture painted in girls' school stories, in which agile pupils shinned up ropes like monkeys, their pigtails flying. In our gym, as the report pointed out, there were the usual rather elderly creaking pieces of equipment: box, horse and bars but no ropes, rings or any other fixed items as, of course, the room had to double up as an art room.

By our arrival in 1959, the swimming pool and loan fund had reached £392 and 'a new swimming bath would be provided when the plans for the new building were finally settled'. It did eventually materialise but too late to be of use to the great majority of those who'd been involved in raising the money for it.

The sporting activities that took place at single-sex schools differed from those in mixed ones. For instance a co-ed might offer football, cricket, netball, hockey, athletics (track and field), swimming, trampoline, indoor gym (horse, ropes, frames etc.), tennis, rounders and field sports. Whereas the minimum sports on offer for the girls at my school were netball, hockey and tennis. Some girls did swimming in place of hockey, and at others there was athletics, rounders and lacrosse in addition. At one of the larger single-sex schools girls took part in the full range of 'girlie' activities: hockey, tennis, netball, rounders, athletics, swimming and gym. Of these, hockey, netball and athletics were played to a high standard at interschool level. Another of the single-sex school in this book provided facilities for 'netball, tennis, rounders, hockey and athletics (including throwing the javelin; minimum supervision – we were trusted). While we were at school in central Oxford we had to walk to our sports ground across the city to the fields where St Catherine's college is now.'

One unhappy former pupil relates:

> I was forced to do netball, hockey, and tennis, but played nothing voluntarily. There were no sports facilities at the school: PE was done in the school hall, and there was just one hard tennis/netball court, so we were bussed out to a suburb to play hockey in the winter and tennis in summer. All sport played in bitterly cold weather, and my hands went white and I could not do up my buttons afterwards. Anyone interested in doing gymnastics properly had to go to an after-school class at the secondary modern school, which had far better facilities. We were made to run around the school dozens of times for long-distance running. Showers were dreaded.

Back at our own school there was a lady who came in part time to teach us religious knowledge (RK). Previously, Ariadne had taught the first two years and Daisy the third year but, says the report, 'standards [were] generally low'. In our second year our two Roman Catholics were allowed to get on with their homework, but we were supposed to read the New Testament during the class. Interestingly, in the lower sixth six of the eleven girls passed RK as an extra O level, so the teaching must have improved considerably.

None of us was discouraged from writing left-handed, in fact it was remarked on that some left-handers were artistically gifted or had good handwriting. You still hear about left-handed children who were bullied and made to feel freaks; some were even hit on the hand with a ruler and in extreme cases had their left hand tied behind their backs.

The only occasion when the mistresses wore gowns was on prize-giving day – and not all of them did then because some weren't graduates and one or two not fully qualified. The days when all teachers in the state section had to hold recognised teaching qualifications were in the future, and it was still possible to gain admittance to a teachers' training college with five O levels. This absence of gowns for the classroom differed from the situation at Lord Williams's where the masters still wore them. This situation gave rise to the (almost certainly fictitious) account of how one of the dreamier of the teachers at that school brought an easel crashing to the floor when he stood up without noticing that an enterprising lad had seized the moment of meditation to pin his gown to the blackboard. Apart from at prize-giving we saw no gowns and, in any case, our teachers wrote on whiteboards. One year, however, the normally self-effacing Miss W. (maths mistress and custodian of the first years) appeared on the stage wearing not one but two hoods, slung side by side.

An examination of the mistresses assembled for the school photographs of 1959, 1962 and 1965 shows a distressing lack of change in their attire. In fact, they could almost be wearing the same – or each other's – outfits. There are the almost universal tweedy suits, or costumes as they were then called, twinsets with or without pearls, and jumpers with twee little Peter Pan collars peeping over the necklines. The hairstyles remain naturally unkempt or show evidence of grown-out perms. The only exceptions to this are the Worthy Bird, who clings stoically to her 'fillet', or headband (which had possibly been the height of fashion when she was a gay young thing), and Daisy, who had a thick head of enviably wavy black hair. It was the teaching staff's business how they chose to appear caught forever on camera, but what does seem unfair is that the 'domestics' appear to have been bundled out of the kitchen mid-task, herded out on to the front lawn still in their overalls and turbans without a chance to comb their hair through or, for all we know, wash the pastry from between their fingers. Small wonder they can't bring themselves to smile.

The colours that most of the teachers wore were equally drab: greys, creams, mousey browns and the occasional olive; nothing colourful or even smart in black. Again there was the one exception: on sunny summer days the maths mistress Miss W. sported 'little girl' dresses in seersucker and gingham with sweetheart necklines which revealed the top of her withering cleavage; attire we considered too young for ourselves, let alone an aged woman of 40-something. These ladies practised what they preached in regard to footwear, for, come rain or come shine, they wore slip-ons or lace-ups to a woman (apart from a couple of weeks at the end of the summer term when one or two of the hardier types ventured out in sandals). Needless to say, it didn't occur to us that they were dressed in a way that was eminently suited to their working life with all its inherent dangers of spilt ink, dropped paint and splinters from desks and chairs. Neither did it cross our minds that they might just have a life outside school, one in which they might wear smart dresses and high heels, and pin up their hair with setting lotion in preparation for a night on the town.

Five

Stayin' In, Bobby Vee, 1961

Unlike at the convent a couple of us had attended, where the nuns had no hesitation in caning the boys, hitting the girls smartly across the outstretched palm with a ruler and clouting miscreants of either sex round the head, punishment for us at secondary school was never corporal. Instead, what little control there was consisted of restrictions, sarcasm and remarks (spoken more in sorrow than in anger), which were calculated to shame us and to make us feel that we had in some way cheated. Corporal punishment was not abolished in state schools until 1986, 1998 in independent ones.

On the whole, we were quite co-operative in regard to the various rules and regulations to which we were subjected – hardly surprising, as they were few and reasonable. Although we didn't give such matters a thought, many were concerned with health and safety, while lots related to our academic progress or lack of it. Some of them would have been easy to flaunt; the world wouldn't really have stopped if we'd been spotted going along the street, minus berets and eating ice cream. Somehow we felt honour-bound to keep up appearances, although one or two of the fifth-formers had the occasional lapse. We would soon have been put in our place in the pecking order, and so we weren't ever tempted to trespass into forbidden parts of school grounds like the dell, sacred to the headmistress herself; the terrace, which was the fifth form's territory; and the island, across which none but the stately feet of the sixth-formers were permitted to tread, and that for arriving and departing only.

We had no class monitors for milk or behaviour. Milk was delivered to the front porch, where the ⅓pint bottles were left in the crate until break time. There was no pressure on us to drink our milk; if we did, we did, and if we didn't, nobody said anything. In regard to behaviour being monitored, our mistresses never left us alone in class so there was no need to appoint such an official. As can be found on the Friends Reunited website:

Miss W was also responsible for the weekly inspection of form rooms. She checked all desks for tidiness. If a desk was not tidy, the lid was left up!! The shame of going into the form-room in the morning and seeing that one's lid was up – and the relief if it was someone else's! Part of the form-room inspection included a display of some sort – flowers or leaves that pupils had to provide – there was some sort of marking including losing marks if there was no display. Pupils were totally involved and felt a sense of shame if they let down the group. I wonder how many schools nowadays could persuade their pupils to be part of this in-school inspection process.

Our misbehaving debut came as early as the end of our first term, when we were marched off to a short carol service at the parish church in the village. An unusual feature of the little building is the set of outside stone stairs which lead to the interior, and we were quite excited by the time we'd settled in. As luck would have it, we were the only people in the church as not even any other pupils had been invited. As we waited expectantly for something to happen, for some reason – which I suspect we couldn't have told you even at the time – something struck somebody as hilarious. It was probably something as simple as a sneeze breaking the hush, but whatever it was started the first person off and then it spread along the rows like wildfire. Not being able to laugh out loud is the surest way to make laughing absolutely essential. Then someone started to hiccup, which naturally made us ten times worse. Needless to say, the carol singing was less than successful. The unfortunate teachers who'd accompanied us didn't know where to put themselves and we were evicted and herded back to school in record time. Whoever had charge of us that day at church had got away lightly. No more was said about it and if we gave it another thought, it was to assume that it had been seen as a bit of childish silliness, best forgiven and forgotten.

It was in this spirit that we were taken to one of the local agricultural shows when we were in the second year. We were taken by coach for our tour of the county show, in the hope that we might learn something about the county in which we lived. In addition to the usual livestock, exhibits, marquees and show rings there was a selection of trade stands. These promoted everything from the Potato and Egg Marketing Boards to the caravans owned by the Big Five banks, from local radio to displays by various tourist organisations. To us these meant attractive brochures and, above all, free samples! We spent literally hours visiting stall after stall picking up leaflets and samples from all over the show-ground, and came back to the meeting place well before the designated time, loaded up with our bounty. Auntie Dottie (who was in charge of us, poor lady, along with a couple of prefects) took one look and sent us straight back to return everything that we'd picked up from the exhibitors. This was done rapidly and under strict supervision so that no one had the chance to dump them behind a tent.

By the May of that year we'd gotten older and bolder. As a rare treat, we were taken to London by coach to see a performance of *She Stoops to Conquer* at the Old Vic. By now we were in that no-man's-land of the third year; 13- and 14-year-olds with attitude, as they say today. Auntie Dottie (who must have decided to forgive, if not forget, her experience at the show) had prepared by reading through the play with us so that we'd know the plot and be able to laugh in all the right places at the eighteenth-century humour, which might otherwise have escaped us. In addition to a trip out to the big city, the icing on the cake was the fact that the lead parts in the show were taken by Tommy Steele (as Tony Lumpkin) and Peggy Mount (as Mrs Hardcastle). Tommy Steele, who needs little introduction today, was a major pop star in 1960 with a string of hit records and several films to his credit. Peggy Mount had been starring in the television comedy series *The Larkins* with David Kossoff and everyone in the country recognised her fog-horn voice. We couldn't wait to get there.

Off we went along the London Road, armed with our packed lunches and a transistor radio. Although London was only a little more than 60 miles away, we made several stops en route to empty out and refill. It was necessary to go into greasy spoons as there were no motorway-type amenities then, but at least there were ladies' toilets – and these ladies' toilets had perfume machines. After putting in your 6*d* and pressing a button you got a powerful spray of a current favourite, such as Max Factor's Primitif and Tweed, more or less in your face. Luckily, nearly all of us had a sixpenny piece handy, and those that didn't borrowed. We were enchanted and stayed well over our allotted time, what with backcombing our hair and spitting into our mascara. Auntie Dottie was not amused by any of it and barked at us sharply as we ambled back to the coach nudging each other and giggling.

A feeling of freedom, together with a sort of herd instinct and the idea of seeing a real live pop star in an hour or so, all went straight to our heads. We were about 14, all girls together, our radio was blaring out (never mind that it faded away under bridges) and all was pretty good in our little world. It wasn't long before we needed to stop again and we were still about an hour away from central London, but nature was calling loud and clear. The last straw, as far as Auntie Dottie was concerned, was when we pulled into a transport cafe. Not surprisingly, there were no perfume dispensers in this stop. Duly relieved, we proceeded to assess the talent and then settle among the lorry drivers, most of whom were young and presentable. As for them, this busload of teenage pulchritude brightened their dreary little day. A cloud of Primitif, albeit somewhat stale by then, still followed wherever we went.

We were on a high and, for once, Auntie Dottie was out of her depth. She was having great difficulty in recapturing her chicks and, not unnaturally, she was worried. Having finally managed it any further trips to the loo were forbidden, even with the threat of damp seats. The fact that she was obviously upset eventually penetrated our consciousness and, faced with her disapproval of us, we suddenly felt small and

cheap. In our silly, juvenile way, we were fond of her and her disappointment in us left a bad taste. We were exceptionally quiet and well behaved as we trooped into the Old Vic and settled down to enjoy the production, which was in fact great fun. One thing we couldn't understand though: why had the female lead (playing opposite Tommy Steele) been given to an unknown, rather dumpy girl with a snub nose? We doubted if we'd ever hear *her* name again. It was Judi Dench.

The journey home was more subdued and we got back in much better time than on the way there. Even so, the damage was done: the staff were alerted to our bad behaviour and a warning given as to the likely consequences of any further trip.

As we got more senior and moved up the school, small acts of non co-operation began to be evident. These usually took the form of not doing the homework set or only completing part of it. Usually this was because the culprit had found more interesting things to do that particular evening or had left it too late. Homework was often started on the way home in the Blue B, where results could be compared with those of our friends or elusive tenses be checked with our seniors. Occasionally set tasks could be exchanged – 'Do my algebra and I'll do your French' – but this was risky as the mistress who'd set the work would soon realise that the unusually correct homework was not, in fact, the efforts of the person whose name appeared on the front of the exercise book.

Another variation of defiance was to learn only part of a vocabulary. The usual instruction was to 'learn half of the vocab on page X'. According to tradition, this was always meant to be the left-hand column, then the right-hand one, but sometimes a couple of bright sparks would take it upon themselves to learn the top half instead. This was taking a bit of a risk, as if a surprise test was set the following morning this deviation was exposed and the offender given a 'DT', or detention. However, this was by no means as unwelcome as it sounds. For a start, because the school was situated at some distance from any form of civilization, everybody was confined to the site during school hours and we were herded into buses and taken away from it as soon as possible afterwards – we could not be kept behind. This meant we weren't missing much if our dinner hours were cut short by incarceration in the sin bin (Room A); indeed there might even be the bonus of time spent in a warm, dry classroom on a winter's day. Once there, under the eagle eye of a junior prefect (who'd also been deprived of her freedom), the work was completed and more often than not any new homework, which had been set during the morning, started. It may of course only be coincidence, but the two most frequent offenders got the highest mark (Grade 1) in the French O-level exam. This taking of liberties with vocabs was confined to French and never to Latin. It never crossed our minds to deviate from usual practice where Bessie was concerned.

Then there was the Semolina Affair. One day for pudding we had a large bowl of barely set, lukewarm semolina which no one was very keen on. The table prefects would try to persuade us to eat a tiny helping, which always ended up smeared round the bowls and that was usually that. This particular day, however, Miss E. was presiding over the school equivalent of high table, at which we found ourselves seated. Someone, who had an upset stomach due to its being the lunchtime after the night before, refused a small bowl containing exactly a one-seventh share of the larger one: 'No, no thank you Miss E., I don't feel at all well, in fact I'd like to leave the table.'

When Miss E., frowned and insisted that she take the bowl, and a rather undignified power struggle followed. This resulted in its being dropped on to the table between them. The girl said nothing but didn't pick up her spoon or take any notice of the semolina. When she repeated this performance with the next girl along, she got exactly the same reaction, as she did with the other three people at the table. The rest of us sat there in silence, wondering if we should eat the semolina (we were still quite hungry and had no objection to the pudding) or refuse it out of solidarity with our friend. She shot us pleading looks. We didn't want to sit there being the only ones keeping Miss E. company, silently spooning up the semolina, so we decided on peer loyalty.

Miss E. went very pale indeed, even paler than usual, so that her pencilled ginger eyebrows stood out against her pink-peach-powdered skin. She started to breathe so heavily so that the air was filled with the sound. Still, she said nothing but went on feeding her face in a self-conscious but genteel way. When she finished her pudding she told us, 'Nobody will leave this table until this food is consumed'. Fair enough. Our hearts hardened. We'd sit there all afternoon if needed be.

Someone muttered: 'Suits me. It's double maths.'

'What's that? If you have something worth saying, please share it with the whole table.'

'I just said that we had double maths at two o'clock,' she was told.

'With the Headmistress,' was added innocently.

The head's maths classes were sacrosanct and to miss one meant you must have some kind of death wish, unless you were already on the way out or prevented from doing so by another teacher, which was unthinkable. In the background the hall was busy as everyone else cleared away their crockery and cutlery to a side table and then put away the collapsible dining tables with satisfyingly loud bangs and crashes. Miss E. knew that she was beaten. By now we were the only ones left in the hall. It was only a minute or two to two o'clock. In the deafening silence she thought the whole business through, decided that it wasn't worth keeping six members of her class away from the head's maths lesson, and backed down.

'Very well, in order not to inconvenience the kitchen staff further you may clear the table and go to your lesson,' she told us graciously. There was, however, the unspoken threat that we hadn't heard the last of this.

'Yessss,' we all said under our breaths. Miss E. glared at us and swept out of the room.

Mums at the time either stayed at home or worked close to home, this, coupled with the fact that the school was relatively remote, meant that truancy was out of the question. We couldn't hang round the house and if we stayed in the town we'd soon have been spotted and reported. As such, once we were at school we had to stay on the premises until it was time for the bus home.

Something which was often resorted to was the mislaying of exercise books after they were supposed to have been given in. For some reason, written work was seldom returned in class, the way of exchanging marked and unmarked homework instead being to leave the piles of books on the top of a set of lockers outside the staff room. Girls would leave their offerings to be collect, marked and duly returned corrected and graded. The more desperate and dishonest among us would swear blind that their books had been among the ones on the lockers, which of course implied that the teacher was the person responsible for its loss.

The penalty for the cardinal sin of being disruptive in class was to be ordered to stand outside the door for the remainder of the session. Nine times out of ten a mistress would ignore a trouble-maker and so not give her the satisfaction of getting attention. On occasions, she would be pushed too far and tell her tormentor to leave the room. This was looked on as something of a sign of weakness on the part of authority, as well as a great opportunity to miss what was obviously not a favourite subject. In theory, the shamed individual might be discovered outside the door as Miss D. came hurrying past the room. If she did, she would stop and demand 'What is the meaning of this?' and expect a suitably penitent explanation and apology. In practice, the girl would amble off to the toilets or take a gentle stroll round the corridors until it was time to get back in position ready to offer a token apology when the class was over and the teacher left the room. If unlucky enough to miscalculate this, and indeed be waylaid by Daisy on her return, an old hand would fake a coughing fit and gasp out the information that she'd left the classroom in order to avoid disturbing the class.

The most frequent cause of friction between the student body and authority was during games lessons, and the most common way of registering displeasure was failing to turn out for hockey practice. As half the winter games' timetable was taken up by netball sessions, and further deductions were made for the Christmas holidays, bad weather and individual sickness, this wasn't very obvious and seldom led to direct confrontation with a games mistress. What did lead to outright disobedience was the introduction of what was euphemistically called cross-country running. The main criticisms which could be levelled against it were that it included no country routes and very little actual running. The main section of the route was along the main road and, as such, was much frequented by leering lorry drivers. Most people got round this by setting off smartly enough along the drive and out of the school grounds, then veering off to the right for a leisurely stroll around the village until it was time to reappear in the drive and run back from the stables and round the island.

Our friend the old PE mistress had no quarrel with this, although she must have known what was going on, but when a new and enthusiastic teacher took over this part of the timetable she provoked a riot. One of her first edicts was that such runs had to be run not walked, let alone strolled, that the route along the main road had to be adhered to with extra diversions across a couple of fields and, by far the worst, the kit was to be pared down from respectable aertex shirt and shorts to a highly embarrassing shirt and navy-blue knickers. This gave a whole new meaning to our mums' worries that we'd be knocked down by a lorry and not be wearing clean knickers. This would certainly not be suggested, let alone allowed, today and we weren't having any of it even then. This flat refusal taught us that if one put one's foot down, there was virtually nothing that any teacher could do about it and it ended up with our picking and choosing what other sporting activities we'd take part in.

Our equivalent of smoking behind the bike sheds was having a puff and a cough in the cloakrooms. This would happen if for any reason, such as a bus being delayed, there had been a chance to avoid assembly. About half a dozen would-be smokers slunk along the corridor and settled in the furthest section of the cloakroom; here there was small chance of their being disturbed and there was an old vase conveniently placed to hold ash. Two or three of the cheaper brands of cigarettes were produced and passed round. At this time it was possible to buy packets containing ten or even two, so that the outlay was nowhere near what it would be today. Nelsons, for example, cost 3/6d (17½p) for twenty and 1/9d (9p) for ten.

Nobody really enjoyed the experience as it was only done for curiosity and bravado; it should be remembered that smoking was universal at this time and had no stigma attached, although of course we'd have been in serious trouble had we been caught for we were under age and had committed one of the worst of all offences: missing assembly. Many types of cigarette came without a filter and those which did were seen as much more sophisticated, probably because they did away with the need to keep pulling loose strands of tobacco and soggy paper from your mouth. Menthol filters were not only trendy but also seen as healthier. The smoking sessions came to an abrupt end when one morning we came into the cloakroom and discovered that our ashtray vase had disappeared, although we never heard anything about the going of it. Fifty years on, when asked by a doctor if she'd ever smoked, a classmate answered without thinking: 'Not since I was at school.'

There was never any insubordination over the wearing of jewellery to school as nobody tried to do so. Ears remained unpierced and fingers unadorned. It's hard to judge what the reaction would have been if anyone appeared with a cross on a chain. The nearest we got to 'jewellery' was cheap and cheerful rings with glass stones (from Woolworth's or the fair), or the type made from silver shillings as love tokens that one or two of the seniors wore hidden away on long chains. For games or PE they'd be taken off and placed carefully in a purse until it was safe to put them on again. No one wore make-up either, as this would have been wasting it. However, if anyone who turned up to a geography lesson with nail polish (even clear or shell pink), they would be packed off to the cloakroom to 'wash that stuff' off their hands. It took months before Miss E. realised that it was not to be got rid off by simple washing, and henceforth offenders would be sent down to the lab to pester Flora for some acetone, coming back reeking of pear drops.

When we were still in one of the junior forms, a peculiar form of bad behaviour took place on Blue B involving a few members of the fourth form. By this time in DS they had graduated from cutting sandwiches and making questionable soup, to producing proper and almost recognisable meals like stews and shepherd's pies. Everything cooked in a DS lesson, successful or not, had to be taken home immediately afterwards. On the various DS days girls could be seen clambering on to buses clutching tins and bowls containing various concoctions, both sweet and savoury. For some reason, these fourth years thought it a huge joke to pour the results of cookery classes out of the bus windows as soon as they reached the main Wheatley road. Sometimes they managed to throw the food clear of the bus but mostly it trickled down the windows where it stuck on to the glass in unappealing patches. I never heard that there were complaints from the bus company, which would have been well within its rights to stop operating the route, under the circumstances. Rather, rumour had it that the food-throwers were put off continuing their hobby when some of their cuisine was blown back inside the bus on a windy day.

More silly than malicious was the reaction to the art mistress's instruction to 'Make a start on painting Marie, while I'm out of the room', when she was called away from an art class. She had no idea that her words would be taken literally, for Marie was one of our classmates. Wearing a soppy smile, Marie sat there quite docilely while two or three of her friends busily applied a layer of foundation, then rouge, lipstick and eye shadow, all made from the most garish colours in our collection of poster paints. When the mistress got back Marie bore more than a passing resemblance to Pocahontas but, to give the teacher her due, she took it all in good heart, making a note to be more careful of how she phrased her instructions in the future. Marie was lucky that she was able to wash the paint off before it irritated her skin or eyes.

Bad language was one sin that we weren't guilty of. It wasn't that we were particularly virtuous, just that we weren't exposed to much swearing in the street and certainly not at home. Needless to say, language on the television and radio was very strictly controlled. We knew most four-letter words, but weren't sure of their exact meaning. In our little world swearing was offensive, not clever or grown up, and blaspheming was confined to the odd 'Oh God!' when seriously provoked. One foul-mouthed first-former, who, incidentally, looked like a blonde angel, was ignored by her schoolmates who refused to be shocked when she started 'effing and blinding', and so she eventually gave up doing it.

It's good to be able to report that there was little or no bullying at the school while we were there, either between older and younger girls or between classmates. Perhaps more strange in an all-female community, bitching and back-biting was kept to a minimum. There were a number of small overlapping groups between which we all moved, which meant that nobody was forced to be in close proximity for too long to someone that she found irritating. For the same reason, it's unlikely that there would have been any racism at the school, although this was never put to the test as we had only a handful of Roman Catholics and no children with known foreign ancestry, let alone any of a different colour.

Discipline and punishments for breaking rules and per-ceived anti-social behaviour differed little from school to school, as did their effect on wrong-doers. They were accepted by us with an 'it's a fair cop' shrug. Detention was by far the most common punishment at all the schools, closely followed by lines. At some schools in this book deterrents such as censure and guilt were in use, and offenders were treated with disapproval and verbal rebukes. Generally, discipline was strict:

> I think we could be given a 'mark' for bad behaviour which would appear on your report but in general, we wouldn't dare to misbehave.

> 'Penalties' were dished out by prefects, which tended to be rather minor punishments. Three penalties, and then you could be given a detention by the staff. To be honest, there wasn't much need.

> We weren't very naughty – being sent to the headmistress if your hair wasn't tied back or had been coloured or back-combed too much. Detention if you failed your French test or history test (maybe you needed to fail 3 tests in a row).

> Lines and detention were the most common forms, mainly lines, but discipline was strong and nobody wanted to feel like a worm if called to attention.

Some schools used order marks as well as detentions; order marks could be put to good use wherever the house system was strong, as getting them was seen as letting down your house. At one school: 'There were detentions held after school. I don't know about corporal punishment – I certainly never received it.' However, in 1918, 14-year-old Archie Leach (who was later to find fame under the name of Cary Grant) was expelled from this school for sneaking into the girls' lavatories.

Another school handed out lines, as well as the intended humiliation of standing outside the classroom door. 'There was also detention, caning for the boys, a stiff "talking to" by the head or deputy head. One set of lines was to write out "I must not put salt in the seniors' water as it might make them ill", a thousand times.' The story of a mistress at this school who lost her temper and stamped so hard that her foot went through the floorboards, resulting in her having to be rescued by a male colleague, has become a legend. This is reminiscent of one elsewhere: 'We had one teacher who threw things e.g. board duster and chalk. She was reputed to have thrown a third-of-a-pint milk bottle, but it went through an open window!' Another student remembered, 'The usual punishment for us was detention, lines or extra subject work. The threat of corporal punishment by caning [for the boys] was there but I cannot remember it ever being used.'

The most unpleasant experience comes from an old, established single-sex school, where punishment was:

> ... mainly order marks and detentions: discipline was psychological and terrifying. (The German teacher was quite mad and used to shake girls until their teeth rattled, but this was probably not official.) It didn't end with the final school gong of the day, as the headmistress used to stand outside as pupils came out checking the length of their skirts, and prefects kept an eye on girls going home on the bus, in case anyone took their hat off or ate a sweet.

As with everything else, today's girls have no idea what they have missed!

Six

Where the Boys Are, Connie Francis, 1961

When reading this section it should be remembered that many grammar schools, including ours, were single sex. The boys that my class came into contact with were either from the boys' grammar school or the slightly older ones from the local College for Rural Crafts. Of course, there were other boys who went to the various secondary modern schools in the area, but they usually went out with girls from the same schools. The situation relating to males aged 18–21 changed significantly on 31 December 1960 when National Service came to an end, although anybody who had deferred doing it was still obliged to go for two years and have their name put on the reserve list for three and a half years.

In regard to our own teenage experiences, one song from the mid-1950s, the popularity of which lasted into the '60s, sums up attitudes at that time very neatly:

Love and marriage, love and marriage,
Go together like a horse and carriage.
This I tell ya, brother, you can't have one without the other.
Try, try, try to separate them, it's an illusion …

The trouble with us was that we tended to believe all those songs that insisted that, if you tried hard enough, you were sure to find the love of your life in the end. Maybe that's because we wanted to believe in romantic love as well as the other kind.

The ways for girls to meet boys in single-sex schools were much more limited than for those who went to mixed ones. These single-sex places were usually grammar schools, but the other type of school, the secondary modern, took both boys and girls. We certainly weren't snobs; we didn't look down on boys who didn't go to the grammar school or the college, we were just more or less unaware that they were around.

Early teen boys tried to grab our attention by childish displays of showing off during games, for instance by hurling a cricket ball in the direction of someone they liked the look of. The thrower then had a chance to show how athletic he was, and it was also a good excuse for going up to the girl to get his ball back. At public dances, though, there were surprisingly few direct pick-ups 'from cold'. Usually a mutual friend was involved or one party would bring over a friend of their own. Often the quarry had already been sighted on a previous occasion before the serious stalking began. School or college dances, or similar events, meant meeting up with the same old crowd nearly every time, even if this circle was fairly wide. Probably because of their novelty value, school friends who were brought along usually managed to pull – sometimes to the annoyance of their hostess. Sixth-form socials certainly did bring about some unexpected pairings.

Another good source of introductions was having family members who'd introduce their friends. An older brother or, even better, two or three, could be a very real asset by the time you were 14. Even if the brother himself didn't make you popular with other girls, who sometimes had dishy male relatives of their own, the sister got to meet a wider selection of the local talent than did the only child. A helpful brother, warned in advance, might even be persuaded to make a friendship on his sister's behalf and send out invitations to the target bloke. One infuriating pest at our school would manage to get to know every new lad first, and would then try to poach him if he was fancied by one of her school-mates. One schoolmate was so annoyed that she made up these lines:

> After the ball is over,
> See her take out her glass eye,
> Put her bee's knees in water,
> Hang up her socks to dry,
> Put her false leg in the corner,
> Hang up her wig on the wall,
> Then what's left goes to bye-byes,
> ******* and all!

(******* being the current male bone of contention between 'the pest' and the composer of this little ditty.)

For us, dating 1960s style couldn't have been much more different from the American teenage scene, according to Neil Sedaka's *Happy Birthday Sweet Sixteen* and *Calendar Girl*. There were no high school proms; no dressing up in cute clothes with a new ribbon in the ponytail, a dab of powder and paint; no waiting to be picked up by one's date dressed in a tuxedo, in Pop's car, with the girl's proud Mom and Pop telling them to be home by eleven then waving goodbye from the veranda. Oh no, nothing so conventional for us.

For those who were confined to school uniforms during the day, weekend and evening wear was very important, but the happy balance between fashion and comfort could be hard to achieve. Sweaters – the bigger the better – were a must. One of the worst fashions of the early 1960s, regarding both comfort and appearance, was the combination of baggy sweater worn hip-length over a full a skirt. This could be obtained by wearing at least one, though usually two and sometimes three, 'can-can' petticoats. The hip-length sweater was supposed to conceal the rolls of surplus petticoat – and puppy fat.

The issuing of invitations was a very casual business, sometimes even off-hand. The accepted process was for one party to enquire, 'Going on Friday night?'

'Might do. You?'

'Might do.'

'See you then.'

'Yeah, see you,' and so what amounted to a date was arranged. Both parties were sure to turn up with a backing group, who may or may not pair off themselves. Their principal purpose, though, was to act as referees; rather like seconds at a duel. Couples who liked each other would just wander off from the main group rather than arrange a definite time and place to meet up in private. Those who disappointed, or were themselves disappointed, soon ended up back with the pack.

When a proper date was arranged at last, it usually took the safe and long-established set-up of a visit to the cinema, dance or concert. In our crowd, a date at the cinema meant shelling out as much as 1/9d per seat, but it was the price you had to pay for a bit of privacy. Contrary from what you might have gathered from boys' conversations, rather than being a bedroom substitute, the pictures were somewhere to get out of the wind and rain (and where you could avoid the strain of keeping up a conversation with someone you hardly knew). When you went out for a drink you risked running into one's mates, and the date ending in a hen party at one end of the bar and a darts match at the other. Going out for a meal was far too expensive; besides, there were very few restaurants informal enough for what we were looking for. Cars were definitely out as very few youngsters held driving licences, let alone owned cars. A few bolder ones had motor-bikes or scooters, which gave them and their conquests a greater field of action, but, human nature being what it is, most boys chose the comfort of the girl's home whenever it was available.

At that age we still had the safety net of the group to fall back on if things went wrong, or if he didn't turn up. There'd always be someone around who'd fancy going to see a film or to a dance, or listening to records, without the unattached being made to feel a gooseberry. By the time we were 16 we were trusted enough to hold our own parties in the rooms which pubs let out for functions. Three or four of us would club together to spread the cost and invite 'new blood' in the way of talent. These events were usually to celebrate someone's birthday or Christmas. Guests weren't expected to bring bottles as the drinks, glasses and plates were pro-vided by the pub and included in the overall price. Most of the drink was alcoholic (beer and cider), although there were soft drinks for those who wanted them. Of course one of our fathers must have made the arrangements with the landlord and have paid him, but this didn't cross our minds. To us it was 'our' party and, as such, up to us who was invited and what they ate, drank and listened to.

Our party fare was the height of 1960s chic, with trendy things like mini pork pies, sausage rolls, cheese straws, scotch eggs and sausages, not forgetting the cheese cubes and pineapple squares on cocktail sticks, sometimes with silver-skin onions, stuck into a grapefruit or large potato. Then there were nibbles: crisps, peanuts, Twiglets and dips (we didn't go so far as quiche and pizza, neither of which anyone was likely to have tried). The party games were our own versions of old favourites, like Postman's Snog, Spin the Bottle and any other excuse for a bit of a giggle. The performing couple went outside the door to do their snogging etc., as it was considered rather bad form to do anything energetic in public – and in any case, they might not fancy so much as a peck on the cheek. Of course, there were always others who'd take advantage and had to be hauled back in again, pink and dishevelled.

When we were all dressed up to the nines we kidded ourselves that nobody would guess that we were still at school. We had darkly outlined doe eyes, which we fondly imagined turned us into Queens of the Nile, just like Elizabeth Taylor in the film *Cleopatra*, worn in conjunction with loads of mascara, Dusty Springfield fashion. This was applied by spitting into the little block in its plastic case, opening our mouths (why did everyone do this?) and brushing on the mascara-and-saliva mix. Our lips we blotted out with foundation (Panstick being the favourite) then palest pink was applied (often silvery lipstick *à la Bardot* in pink pearl or pearly peach); all this was in startling contrast to the muck clinging round our eyes. Strangely enough, everybody made fun of singer Kathy Kirby's shiny lipstick which was several years in advance of its time.

Outside school shoes were universally the pointed-toe stiletto, apart from those for the late middle-aged and elderly.

Such a menace did this type of heel become that they were often banned from wooden flooring. Some tourist attractions, fearing for their floors and their incomes alike, hit on the idea of providing soft flat slippers like giant bread rolls, which their lady visitors were obliged to pad around in. It was also possible to invest in a pair of plastic heel guards. These were about 2in long and ended in a rounded heel which covered the spike of the stiletto. Recently, I was presented with a pair of these by someone who was totally at a loss as to their identity. They would make a suitable item for a quiz show. Toes of shoes eventually became so extreme that they were known as winkle-pickers. These came with or without stiletto heels, indeed some were almost flat, and came in laced-up styles which just managed to scrape into the category of school uniform footwear.

In the early winter of 1963 some adventurous types appeared at parties in clothes and shoes which were the complete opposite of what we had all been wearing, in slightly modified forms, for the last three years or more. This was the vanguard of the Mod look: very demure with Granny shoes (that is, with stumpy little heels known as Louis or lavatory heels) and dresses which were cut to fall softly like a child's party dress, often with lace collars and cuffs and in all-over patterns like sprigs or tiny spots.

Whenever we could get as far afield as one of the larger towns, Woolworth's cosmetics counter was a prime haunt, for its contents were just within our very limited budget and, just as relevant, we could try it all out free of charge. In the early 1960s the Rimmel 'Beauty on a budget' range was launched with the slogan:

All that's best for beauty, all at 1/3d, enables the career girl in a hurry to choose a cosmetic wardrobe in the minimum

time, the housewife with a limited budget to afford the best in cosmetics, and the teenager to experiment with new fragrances, new make-up, and new shades! All at 1/3d.

Apart from the mascara, among the favourites were sticks of startling mauve and green glittering eye shadow.

One of the biggest hits of 1961 was the Brook Brothers' *War Paint*. The lines, which must have aroused a good deal of sympathy with young males at the time, were:

> *In your lipstick, powder and paint,*
> *All dressed up like what you ain't,*
> *You dye your hair a different shade,*
> *We're going to a movie not a masquerade,*
> *and*
> *You may think that you look cute,*
> *But I don't think it's funny when you ruin my suit!*

The same duo recorded another hit, *Ain't Gonna Wash for a Week*, which also rang a few bells.

We also had great fun trying out every perfume tester we could lay our hands on. If we had to stay in the town we mooched around the local chemist's shop, but this was nowhere near as rewarding.

The one fashion accessory which everyone could afford was jewellery, usually bought from Woolworth's or the local chemist's. In this, we showed about as much finesse as a magpie. The preference was for large, dangling clip-on or screw-on earrings, which contained 'diamonds' that caught the light. Dangling earrings were sometimes heavy enough to pinch the lobes and turn them an unflattering shade of beetroot.

Imagine then, if you will, a bird's nest atop a deathly pale face, with no lips apart from a thin metallic strip and black eyes reminiscent of a silent movie star. Add an over-long sweater, usually 'borrowed' from an unsuspecting male who would later complain about its being returned smelling like a 'tart's boudoir', as the saying went. Set these on a sort of flowered umbrella with a very uneven hem and watch the whole ensemble totter along on the latest stiletto heels. Then you will have some idea of what constituted our idea of feminine beauty in the early 1960s.

As with past, and no doubt future, generations, the first attempts at physical exploration took place in doorways, bus and park shelters, and, in our case, the porch of the parish church. They came with the usual corny comments about warming hands and warnings about stretching the girls' sweaters. Hands-on experience, though, was strictly limited by just about everyone to the bits of the body that could decently appear unclothed in public or on the beach. Any further liberties were looked on as cheating until the relationship had been put on some sort of serious footing. When this point was reached, however, privacy became really important. Once the introductions were out of the way and the boy got his feet under the table, a room was earmarked for what the older generation called the 'courting couple'. All this depended on the relationship having survived that first invitation to come round to tea. From then onwards, parents would act on the 'better the devil you know' principle.

Front rooms definitely had their advantages over shop doorways and church porches, especially in winter. The would-be lovers could be all but certain that their records and radio would make sure of their being uninterrupted by the rest of the family. Parents didn't want to hear endless replays of the top twenty hits, which meant that adults would stay at a safe distance. Even better was the evening, perhaps only once a week or month, when you could have the house to yourselves with the older generation off to bingo or down the local club or pub. Best of all, though (said those in the know) was the delicious quiet of Saturday morning when the boyfriend had stayed overnight, pure and alone, in the spare room. You could go in to say good morning, take him a mug of tea and have a little cuddle. Youth and innocence – without the sweating, panting, groaning conclusion! Few, if any of us, had gained experience of that sort of thing as yet.

We were given no sex education at school, and the majority had very little at home, until it could no longer be avoided. The nearest we did get was centred round the O level human biology & hygiene syllabus, which, virtually without fail, would set a question on either the male or female human reproductive system. To a woman, we could draw and label both systems and list the functions of the individual parts; the problem occurred when it came to working out exactly how they worked together! We were even shown a very clinical film on the subject, but the main query remained as to how the penis, looking just like a tap, could be persuaded to realign itself sufficiently to enter the vagina and stay there. The adjectives 'flaccid', 'arousal' and 'erect' were of course never mentioned.

With us there was little or no sleeping around; any girl who risked 'going too far' with a boy who wasn't her regular boyfriend (say, to 'Number 5' and beyond) was labelled a tart by the girls just as much as by the boys; probably even more so by the girls. The 'table of action' went as follows:

1 See a boy/girl and like him/her
2 Get to know him/her
3 Hold hands
4 Kiss
5 Upstairs outside
6 Downstairs outside

7 Upstairs inside
8 Downstairs inside
9 It
10 Nine months later …

Going to 'Number 9' was generally frowned upon, except in a relationship which seemed to have a very promising future indeed. Even under these circumstances the girl was running a great risk, partly on account of the likely loss of 'respect' but, first and foremost, of pregnancy.

A film that is very much of its time (1962) is *A Kind of Loving*, which explores the very topical themes of ignorance and embarrassment leading to unwanted pregnancy and the outcome of the resulting 'having to get married'. Opinions about pregnant brides ranged from their being hussies who had deliberately trapped their man, to being unlucky enough to get 'caught'. Ever-so-slight envy on the part of her schoolmates rapidly changed to self-righteous relief when one such newly-wed found herself exiled to a run-down cottage in the middle of nowhere, with no shops within miles, dependent on a well for all her water and a baby very much on the way. Only a matter of months earlier the greatest of her problems had been the results of her mock O levels. Even more unlucky (at least in the short term), were those girls who took a chance, became pregnant and did not have the chance to marry the father for a variety of reasons. There was no history locally of girls being sent away to institutions who would treat the mothers-to-be as criminals, or even mental defectives, and put the babies up for adoption, as happened in other parts of the country. Pregnant girls with no prospects of marriage might find themselves sent off to stay with a tolerant relative until they had given birth, after which they returned as if from an extended holiday. The community, at least in front of the family in question, would keep up the pretence and the procedure came to be referred to as 'going to stay with your granny'. Fortunately, teenage pregnancies were rare; the concept of bringing shame to your family being a sufficient deterrent. So there it was. Love and respect versus the biological urges. Even in that day and age, when a woman's body was beginning to be seen as hers to do what she liked with, you still had to tread carefully.

To be fair to the boys, they were in a quandary when out on a date. If they went too fast they got the reputation of being 'randy', which might be fine among their peers but meant that girls wouldn't want to find themselves alone with them. On the other hand, if they didn't make a move they were in danger of being labelled a baby or a mother's boy, or, much worse, a 'queer'.

At our prize-giving in 1958 the representative of the board of governors said, 'Surely if it is true love it will stand the delay of your training; if it is not, the sooner you discover so the better, and believe me, it had better be true and strong to stand the vicissitudes of married life'. She ended by reminding us that young married women now had to make some contribution to the family finances and urged, 'Take full advantage of the chances available to you now!'

Seven

A Handful of Songs, Tommy Steele, 1957

It's hard to remember when pop music became a central part of your life, both at school and at home, and equally difficult to know when it stopped being so as your priorities gradually change. During these school years it formed a large part of our conversation and we were most competitive in being the first to spot a particular singer or group; it's certain that nobody wanted to be the last to know about the latest musical fad. For teenagers all over the country, schooldays were illuminated by a series of recordings. These meant so much to us at the time and came to represent those years; they can still bring a smile and a tear some fifty years on. Not all of them were songs, in fact there were a lot of instrumentals.

Up in Liverpool in 1958, the year that we started grammar school, John, Paul and George were forming The

Quarrymen, but nobody would hear of them for four years, by which time they'd become The Beatles. The Shadows were still the Drifters and two of the best-selling records were Perry Como's *Magic Moments* and *Move It*, the first hit from a soulful and rather plump teenager called Cliff Richard.

The faintest hint of dampness in the air over lunchtime was eagerly exploited. A scout would be sent outside to test the weather and, needless to say, she always reported that there was rain about. We had to wait until all the tables and forms had been cleared away in the hall and then we'd get out the portable record player that was used for music classes. One memorable day in 1961 someone discovered a few ancient plastic records, one of which was *You're Driving Me Crazy*, the Temperance Seven's new version of which was currently in the Hit Parade. Someone always brought in a couple of singles on the off chance, and there were usually one or two more in lockers. The most-played ones stand out as being Chubby Checker's *Let's Twist Again* and Gerry and the Pacemakers' *How Do You Do It?* and *I Like It*, backed up by plenty of The Shadows and, of course, all The Beatles' latest. What just about summed up our feelings when we were in the third year, though, was hearing Helen Shapiro belt out *Don't Treat Me Like a Child*.

The records that we treasured were rigid, breakable, easily chipped and scratched by a blunt or jumping needle and heavy to carry around. Treasured loans returned and found damaged in this way could immediately end the most beautiful of friendships, and refusals to lend aborted many a promising one. Anyone who hasn't been through the agony of having a favourite record can have no concept of the joy of compact discs. The oldest singles were 78s (revolutions per minute), later replaced by the smaller 45s. There were also EPs (extended play, with four tracks) and LPs (long-playing

33.5rpm records), also called albums. Both of the latter came in cardboard covers with designs, which sometimes became works of art in themselves. These might be pinned on the wall like posters as a form of decoration, especially at parties.

We bought our records from a number of outlets, such as the stall at the market that sold 78s from cardboard boxes. Inside the covered market in the city there was a booth which stocked a wide selection of records, from old standards to the latest pop LPs. In most towns there was an electrical shop which sold a limited number of LPs, as well as radiograms, record players and radios. There were also specialist music shops where you could go into sound-proofed booths and listen to what you wanted to hear, even if you had no intention of buying. The record centre advertised in the local paper, offering to send off new releases by post. In the larger towns there was a branch of Woolworth's, who did their own cover versions of chart hits for a smaller charge. One of the most exciting places to visit was the indoor market at Blackpool, where all the latest records were available much more cheaply and formed part of many a holidaymaker's luggage.

Right at the top of the present list for any self-respecting teenager was a trannie (transistor radio) and there were plenty of radio programmes which indulged our craving for pop music. These had started as early as 1955 with *Pick of the Pops*, the best-known presenter being Alan Freeman who took over in 1961. *Easy Beat* with Brian Matthew began in 1959. On television, *Cool for Cats* with Kent Walton, which ran from 1956 to 1961, was a once-a-week, fifteen-minute rundown of the latest records. *Six-Five Special*, so called because it was broadcast at 6.05 p.m. on Saturdays in 1957–58, was the first rock and jazz live show, presented by Pete (later Peter) Murray. The following year *Oh Boy!* (1958–59) featured live performances by top British and

American performers like Tommy Steele, Cliff, Marty Wilde and Billy Fury. Much more long-lasting was *Juke Box Jury*, which started in 1959 and went on until 1967. It consisted of a panel, hosted by David Jacobs, with four celebrities who commented on new releases and voted them a hit or a miss.

Two years later, in 1961, ITV launched *Thank Your Lucky Stars*, which was more like a variety show with a high concentration of the emerging Merseybeat groups – notably Billy J. Kramer and the Dakotas, and Gerry and the Pacemakers. Before *Lucky Stars* finished in 1966, it saw a host of presenters who would become household names, including Keith Fordyce, Jimmy Savile, Pete Murray and Jimmy Young. Among the leading performers of the day were Tom Jones, Lulu, The Ronettes and The Supremes. A popular part of the show was 'Spin a Disc', in which a panel of record-buyers judged new releases with a score of one to five. In 1962 a 16-year-old participant called Janice Nicholls created a catchphrase with her approving 'Oi'll give it foive' delivered in a Black Country accent. The Beatles performed their latest single, *Paperback Writer*, on the very last programme, *Goodbye Lucky Stars*, on 25 June 1966.

'The Weekend Starts Here', the introduction to *Ready Steady Go* (*RSG*), which went out live at 6 p.m. on Friday nights from 1963 to 1966, summed up our enthusiasm for the next couple of days. Its first signature tune was *Wipe Out* by the Surfaris, but was replaced by Manfred Mann's *5-4-3-2-1*. The launch of the programme coincided with the British beat explosion and youth culture, in which The Rolling Stones, The Who and, of course, The Beatles played leading parts. The official presenter was DJ Keith Fordyce but the real celebrity was co-host Cathy McGowan, famous for her deep fringe, long shiny hair and even longer legs, who later gained the title of 'Queen of the Mods'. The BBC's *Top of the Pops*, which started in 1964, hosted by Jimmy Savile, showcased top chart hits and British groups. The programme saw the first television appearances of, among others, Eric Burdon and the Animals, the Kinks, Donovan and The Pretty Things, as well as well-established American artistes making their British television debuts.

Those who got the opportunity to see their idols live on stage jumped at the chance. The cost was nowhere near as much as it is nowadays, and stars on tour would visit cinemas that put on shows, not just the larger theatres and arenas. One of these was the Odeon in a nearby town where we'd been to see many a pantomime when we were children. Among the artistes performing there were Bobby Vee and Buddy Holly's former backing group, The Crickets. Billy Fury must have set many female hearts aflutter when he played Aladdin at the theatre in 1966, but by then we were far too old for that kind of entertainment and wouldn't have even known that he was appearing. It was too far to go up to London and back afterwards, and no one would have dreamt of staying there overnight. However, we would take full advantage of cramming in as many concerts as we could when we were on holiday, especially in Blackpool. The leading venues there were the theatres on the three piers and the Winter Gardens. Among the shows taken in during a visit to the Illuminations were the Swinging Blue Jeans, Frank Ifield and Manfred Mann. An unforgettable memory is of Paul Jones, dressed entirely in black on a darkened stage, performing *Smokestack Lightning*.

Sophisticated as we thought of ourselves, what we liked the very best of all were the straightforward romantic numbers, even more so if they were about people of a similar age to ourselves instead of dodderers in the 1920s and '30s. The 1957 hit, of which there were several versions, was *Young Love, First Love*:

They say for every boy and girl,
There's just one love in this old world,
And I, I kn-ow, I, I, I've found mine.
The heavenly touch of your embrace,
Tells me no one will take your place,
A, A, A, A, ever in my heart.

At Christmas 1958 we were singing along to the Teddy Bears' *To Know Him Is to Love Him*, which struck us as highly romantic, even though we hadn't as yet met a 'Him' that we could fall in love with. Ricky Nelson's 1959 hit, *There'll Never Be Anyone Else but You*, although very popular, was nevertheless parodied by our little gang who substituted 'You' for 'Hugh' as that was the name of a current boyfriend.

In June 1959 the highly appropriate *A Teenager in Love* ('One day I feel so happy, the next I feel so sad') was taken into the charts by no less than three artistes: Craig Douglas, Marty Wilde and Dion & the Belmonts. That August, Craig Douglas had a No 1 hit with *Only Sixteen*, with other versions by Sam Cooke and Al Saxon reaching No 23 and No 24, respectively. *Heartbeat*, another Buddy Holly hit of 1959, was destined to be a classic when it became the theme song for a television series. It was particularly poignant because Holly had been killed a plane crash earlier that year; a tragedy that would inspire Don McLean's 1972 hit *The Day the Music Died*. Buddy Holly's posthumous *True Love Ways* (1960) was a really dreamy background for spending a cosy evening with the beloved:

Throughout the days,
Our true love ways,
Will bring us joys to share
With those who really care …

Later, The Beatles' *There's a Place* (1963) and *Things we said Today* (1964) expressed similar thoughts. The Springfields' *Island of Dreams* takes one 64-year-old straight back to 1962, when she told her 17-year-old boyfriend that she didn't think that she would ever want to get married. He proposed immediately and she accepted after only five seconds thinking about it.

Cilla Black's hit *You're My World* (1964) and Mary Wells' *My Guy* of the same year summed up how we felt when all was going well, as did Sonny and Cher's *I Got You Babe* the following year:

Cher: *They say we're young and we don't know,*
We won't find out until we grow.

Sonny: *Well I don't know if all that's true*
'Cause you got me, and baby I got you.

Because a number of us had boyfriends who lived quite a distance away (boarders), songs about long-distance romance had a definite appeal. Being parted from the loved one for the summer vacation was described in three American 1962 hits: Brian Hyland's *Sealed with a Kiss*, Carole King's *It Might as Well Rain until September* and Ketty Lester's *Love Letters*. The Beatles, too, knew all about separation. In 1962 they released *P.S. I Love You*:

Treasure these few words till we're together,
Keep all my love forever, P.S. I love you.

The LP *Please Please Me*, which came out in 1963, included *A Taste of Honey*, which contains the words:

Yours was the kiss that awoke my heart,
There lingers still, 'though we're far apart,
That taste of honey … tasting much sweeter than wine.
I will return, yes I will return,
I'll come back (he'll come back) for the honey (for the
honey) and you.

The single of the same year, *All My Loving*, declared:

Close your eyes and I'll kiss you,
Tomorrow I'll miss you,
Remember I'll always be true,
And that while I'm away
I'll write home every day
And send all my loving to you.

The return of the loved traveller was celebrated in two more 1963 hits, the Angels' *My Boyfriend's Back* and Billy Fury's *Like I've Never Been Gone*. Finally, that year also saw the release of a song which caused parted lovers' blood to run cold, Gene Pitney's *Twenty-Four Hours from Tulsa*, in which the singer relates to his girlfriend how he's met 'somebody' new while on his way to see her and that he can 'never, ever, come home again'.

One of the most iconic songs of the early 1960s was the Shirelles' 1961 hit, *Will You Love Me Tomorrow?*

Tonight you're mine completely
You give you love so sweetly
Tonight the light of love is in your eyes
But will you love me tomorrow?

There are even more songs about unrequited love, however; Buddy Holly's *It Doesn't Matter Any More* (1958) summed up its hopelessness. In retrospect, the phrase 'now and forever 'til the end of time' is a bit disturbing. Roy Orbison was one of the best exponents with *Only the Lonely* (1959), as we were all lonely at some time in our insecure little bubbles, and *Love Hurts* (1961) as anyone who was young and without a boyfriend did when everyone else around had one, at least for that particular week. *Rubber Ball* with its lyrics about a heart that was 'bounced around' was a hit for Bobby Vee in 1960, and both Marty Wilde and The Avons made successful versions the following year.

One of the most-played records of the early 1960s was Del Shannon's *Runaway* of 1961, with one of the falsetto passages which were typical of the time. Billy Fury's *Halfway to Paradise* (1961) expressed all the feelings of disappointment felt when someone we fancied treated us like a friend. Billy Fury started recording in the late 1950s but didn't make it big until the '60s. He suffered from heart problems and in 1983 collapsed when returning home from the recording studio, he died the next morning aged 42. Cilla Black's first No 1, *Anyone Who Had a Heart* (1964), similarly speaks of the frustration and longing of falling in love with someone who didn't want to know about it.

The sultry Eden Kane's hits *Well I Ask You* (1961) and *Forget Me Not* (1962) bring back the memory of how a picture cut out of a teenage girl's magazine and stuck up on a bedroom picture rail provoked jealousy from a boyfriend who didn't like the idea of the pop star looking down on his beloved as she undressed. The girl objected to his rash comment that he found Susan Maughan attractive, so they didn't play *Bobby's Girl* either. On the subject of jealousy, in the early 1960s pop heroes weren't supposed to be married as this destroyed their image of being 'available'. Many of them kept even their relationships secret and the news that John Lennon had married Cynthia in August 1962 was treated as something verging on a scandal. By the middle of the decade, everybody had grown up and accepted that these things happened so that every detail of stars' romances and marriages was seized eagerly.

Joe Brown & the Bruvvers' *A Picture of You* (1962) and *That's What Love Will Do* (1963) tell of regrets for what might have been, the second being about the girl that he couldn't manage to forget. Billy Fury's *Last Night was Made for Love* is along the same lines; it ends:

> I know there'll never be another time
> Another magic night to make you mine,
> There gone forever, sad but true,
> Last night was made for love,
> But where were you?

Chad and Jeremy's *Yesterday's Gone* (1964) was another gentle lament, this time for a love that had waned with the summer, but it does end with the hope that it might return the following year. In 1963 Freddie and the Dreamers' *If You Gotta Make a Fool of Somebody* was very much a novelty when performed live, for Freddie leapt around all over the stage while singing all of his numbers.

Among the pleas to reconsider, one of the most successful (at least commercially) was The Allisons' *Are You Sure?* These two youngsters, who were discovered on a talent show, were in the charts for weeks and went on to come second in the Eurovision Song Contest of 1961 when representing the UK. When the worst happened and you got dumped, you were in good company. In 1960 even Elvis wasn't immune to being in the position of hoping for a second chance with *Are You Lonesome Tonight*? Similarly, Helen Shapiro asked a friend to *Tell Me What He Said* in 1962, in the hope that she'd soon be *Walking Back to Happiness*. It was bad enough when the beloved was unfaithful, but if it happened publicly everyone could sympathise with Lesley Gore's *It's my Party*, a 1963 track which appears very frequently in 1960s compilations. When discarded, few, if any of us, would have been noble enough to echo the sentiments of Bobby Vee in *Take Good Care of my Baby* and *Run to Him* (both 1961) or the two Beatles' tracks from their LP *Please Please Me*: *Anna (Go to Him)* and *Misery*. Even The Shadows were at it with *Don't Make my Baby Blue* in 1965:

That little girl's an angel,
And it hurts me to set her free,
So you'd better take good care of her
'Cause she still means the world to me

The female side of things was Mary Wells' *Oh, Little Boy (Look What you've Done to Me)*, the 1964 B-side of her wonderful *My Guy*. The greatest of all the break-up, make-up records was of course The Beatles' *She Loves You*, with its unforgettable 'yeh, yeh, yeh', that made its way all round the world.

It goes without saying that there were dozens of songs that you automatically joined in with that made you glad to be young and alive. Jerry Keller's *Here Comes Summer* (1959) still conjures up sunny days of freedom to do whatever you felt like doing. Another 1959 hit, Eddie Cochran's sing-along *C'Mon Everybody*, preceded a disaster similar to Buddy Holly's as on 17 April 1960 Cochran, aged only 21, was killed in a taxi crash in Chippenham, Wiltshire. Gene Vincent was also seriously hurt in the accident. In 1961, a second Eddie Cochran posthumous belter was *Weekend*. Hearing Johnny Kidd & the Pirates' *Shakin' All Over* now recalls hearing it blaring out over the loudspeakers at the fair in 1960 while being shaken up on the Octopus.

Girlie titles, Johnny Burnett's *You're Sixteen*, Neil Sedaka's *Calendar Girl* and *Happy Birthday Sweet Sixteen*, were big hits in 1960–61, when we were that age ourselves, although regrettably nothing like the peaches and cream, satin and lace-wearing little dolls in the songs. In 1961, hits that expressed the joy of being part of a couple were Connie Francis' *Where the Boys Are* and Bobby Vee's *Walking with my Angel*, with its distinctive sound of footsteps. Over the festive season in 1962 we went *Rockin' Around the Christmas Tree* with Brenda Lee, although it's doubtful if any of us ever had the chance to try some pumpkin pie.

We came out of the cinema in 1963, after watching Cliff and The Shadows in the film *The Young Ones*, with the warning ringing in our ears that:

> *Young dreams should be dreamed together,*
> *And young hearts shouldn't be afraid,*
> *To live, love, while the flame is strong,*
> *Cause we may not be the young ones very long …*

This was something that became apparent not long afterwards when we were out in the wide world as little fishes in a very big pond. The words 'tomorrow sometimes never comes' proved only too accurate for two of us, one of whom died of a tumour and the other as the result of a car crash shortly after starting his first job.

The year 1961 was the year of the twist, a dance craze popularised by Chubby Checker's *Let's Twist Again*, although his original record, *The Twist*, had been released the previous summer it had failed to make much impact. Other artistes making twisting records included Petula Clark, Frankie Vaughan and even Frank Sinatra. Another dance copied The Shadows' walk, which has been described as consisting of 'a 3 step walk contained within a 60-60-60 degree triangle formation with a reverse right-heel back-kick with optional can-can finale'. In a sort of line dance, we'd walk forward and back during certain tracks such as *FBI*, *Atlantis* or *Kon-Tiki*. Little Eva's *The Loco-Motion* (1962) gave instructions on how it was to be performed, but in reality the song came before the dance and when it became a hit, a dance had to be invented to go with it. The dances mentioned in Brian Poole and The Tremeloes' 1963 hit *Do You Love Me? (Now that I can Dance)* are the mashed potato and the twist. The same year, Chris Montez's *Let's Dance* quotes the twist, the stomp and the mashed potato – but neither of the other two really caught on, certainly not to the extent that the twist did. The Swinging Blue Jeans had a hit with *Hippy Hippy Shake* in 1963 but, once again, there was no such dance to go with the record when it first came out.

For a couple of years at the start of the 1960s disaster songs were in vogue. Amongst these was *Ebony Eyes*, the Everly Brothers' 1960 B-side of *Walk Right Back*:

Then I felt a burning break deep inside
And I knew the heavenly ebony skies,
Had taken my life's most wonderful prize,
My beautiful Ebony Eyes

This also contained the spoken words 'They may have run into some turbulent weather', which we learned, parrot-fashion, and would solemnly say 'looks like turboolent weather' to each other every time rain threatened.

Probably the best-known tragedy record was Ricky Valance's *Tell Laura I Love Her*, about a boy who enters a car race in order to win enough money to marry his sweetheart but is killed when his car crashes. Some cynic remarked that at least he'd remain hers for eternity instead of going off with someone else as soon as he had the chance, like boys in real life did. Also parodied was our invention, *Tell Gordon I Love Him* (1961), which instead of 'Tell Laura not to cry, my love for her will never die', ended 'Tell Gordon not to get drunk, my love for him will do a bunk'. As old man Steptoe used to say, 'Callous little bleeders!' Another over-the-top, tragedy song was Johnny Leyton's *Johnny, Remember Me*:

> *I hear the voice of my darlin',*
> *The girl I loved and lost a year ago.*

Its original lyrics were even worse, 'the girl I loved died a year ago'. The same artiste had a hit later in 1961 with *Six White Horses and a Golden Chariot*, which had the words:

> *There was laughter and love we were happy,*
> *Till a tornado swept her away,*
> *I lost sight of my darlin',*
> *In an angry cloud of flame.*

A feature of those years was the number of comic songs that made it into the Hit Parade. In 1958 Bernard Bresslaw, the 6ft 7in-tall star of *The Army Game* and several *Carry On* films, released *Mad Passionate Love*, which turned out to be about a couple of amorous birds. The B-side was *You Need Feet*, a parody of Max Bygraves's *You Need Hands*. The following year saw Lonnie Donegan's *Does Your Chewing Gum Lose Its Flavour (On The Bedpost Overnight?)* and the Avon's *Seven Little Girls Sitting In The Back Seat*. Then, in 1960, there was an epidemic of humorous titles: Perry Como's *Delaware*, Max Bygraves' *Fings Ain't Wot They Used to Be*, Donegan's *My Old Man's A Dustman (Ballad Of A Refuse Disposal Officer)*, Peter Sellars and Sophia Loren's *Goodness Gracious Me* and *Bangers and Mash*, Anthony Newley's *Strawberry Fair*, Andy Stewart's *Donald Where's Your Troosers?*, Charlie Drakes' *My Boomerang won't come back*, Bernard Cribbins' *Hole in the Road* and Right Said Fred, Mike Sarne and Wendy Richard's *Come Outside* (this was the same Wendy Richard who featured in *Are You Being Served?* and, later still, starred as Pauline Fowler in *EastEnders*). These types of records became hits and generated several catchphrases, which are still remembered, but as we couldn't dance or dream to them we weren't hugely interested.

Not all of the hits of the 1950s and '60s were vocals, though; in fact a good number were instrumental. The year 1960 brought the John Barry Seven's *Hit and Miss*, which was the theme tune for *Juke Box Jury*. Another instrumental, pianist Russ Conway's *Royal Event*, coincided with the birth of Prince Andrew. He was the first child to be born to a reigning monarch for 103 years and the fact that the queen was pregnant at the (to us) advanced age of 34 was almost beyond belief. Russ Conway had a string of hits, as did guitar experts Bert Weedon, Duane Eddy and the jazz bands of Acker Bilk and Kenny Ball.

Many of these instrumentals weren't rock and pop numbers at all but 'proper music', as parents would have called it. Some were from films, like the *Theme from a Summer Place* which was a hit for both Percy Faith & His Orchestra and the Norrie Paramour Orchestra, and also James Darren's *Because They're Young* from the film of the same name, all of which came out in 1960. Ferrante & Teicher's *Exodus* (*Theme from 'Exodus'*) followed in 1961. Mr Acker Bilk had a big hit with *Stranger on the Shore* in 1961 and two years later with *A Taste of Honey*, which was the instrumental equivalent of The Beatles' song. The Norrie Paramour Orchestra had another success with the *Theme from Z Cars* (1962), from the hugely popular television police series which was set in Liverpool.

As part of the entertainment at a fete in 1960, school friends Jen and Deidre were choreographed in an Apache dance, dressed in clothes to represent a genuine Left Bank Parisian floor show. This involved Jen, dressed in trousers, striped jersey, beret and pencilled-in moustache, dragging Deidre, in a shiny skirt slit to her thighs, across the non-too-clean floor of the hall. What ruined it for us onlookers was not the dancing itself, but the fact that the record to which it was performed was nothing at all like The Shadows' current hit, which we'd all been expecting.

The Tornados released a very topical record in 1962. It was called *Telstar* after the successful satellite that had recently been launched. The record cleverly imitates the satellite as it comes close at the start and then fades away from the listener. In 1962 The Shadows' *Wonderful Land* stayed at the No 1 position in the UK for longer than any other single during the whole of the 1960s (eight weeks). More unusual than the straight instrumentals were the versions of classical favourites which were turned into rock hits and given wacky titles. Early examples were *Hoots Mon* (*Wi' a Hundred Pipers an' a' an' a'*) by Lord Rockingham's XI and *Beatnik Fly* (a rocked-up *Blue tail Fly* aka *Jimmy Crack Corn*) by Johnny and the Hurricanes in 1958. In 1960 the Piltdown Men had hits with *McDonald's Cave* (*Old McDonald's Farm*), *Piltdown Rides Again* (*William Tell Overture*) and

Goodnight Mrs Flintstone (*Good Night Ladies*). B. Bumble & The Stingers with *Nut Rocker* (*The Nutcracker Suite*) and The Cougars with *Saturday Night at the Duck pond* (*Swan Lake*) followed on in 1963.

So many of our teenage records have been re-released and covered by younger artistes over the years that they have become classics, something that we would have thought impossible way back then.

Eight

Food, Glorious Food!, Oliver!, 1960

Due to the fact that separate shops sold different items, shopping, especially food shopping, was a lengthy business until small, self-service shops began to increase in number in the early 1960s. Apart from newsagents, which opened for a few hours, all shops were closed on Sundays and Bank Holidays, as well as during the lunch hour and on early closing days, which varied from place to place. Fortunately for my class, rationing finished in July 1954 and had left no impression on us.

Milk was nearly always delivered to the doorstep, like the post, and in glass, not plastic, bottles. Containers like miniature crates held 2, 4 or occasionally 6 pints. Some containers had a device with a pointer indicating how many pints were needed. Bottles came with different coloured foil caps to show what type of milk they contained: gold top was added cream and quite unusual; silver top was whole milk; red, semi-skimmed (also unusual); and red and silver stripes, standard. Some people bought terracotta covers for the milkman to put over their bottles; in the summer it kept the sun off them and in the winter stopped the blue tits from pecking the foil tops off. When it was very cold the cream on the milk would freeze and form a plug, which extended out of the neck of the bottle and dislodged the top. Bread came in enormous baskets slung over the arm of the delivery man or boy. If bread was bought in a bakery, they might wrap it in a single sheet of tissue paper. It was never sealed and, once in the house, lived in a breadbin. Loaves of bread were also on sale in mini-marts and supermarkets, and these were wrapped in waxed paper that was difficult to close.

Meals were generally home-made with fresh ingredients, although there were of course tins of vegetables and fruit, dried foodstuffs and a limited amount of frozen food available. Most homes had fridges but there were very few separate domestic freezers. An amusing illustration of the novelty of frozen foods is the story of two mothers who went into a greengrocer's to choose treats for tea from the small freezer which had just been installed in the corner of the shop. Having bought several corns on the cob and a box of chocolate éclairs, they sat down to enjoy them only to discover with great disappointment that not only did the contents of both packages need to be defrosted, the corn also had to be cooked. Packet meals such as Vesta curries were also on sale in the more go-ahead grocers. These contained bags of dried rice and the dehydrated ingredients for making the sauce which passed for curry. Paella, sweet and sour and chow mien were also available. All had to be boiled in a bag at great danger to fingers; nine times out of ten the contents hadn't been sufficiently reconstituted but by then it was too late to put them back in the water as the bags had been opened. This didn't put us off, though, as we felt ourselves to be terribly cosmopolitan to be eating them at all.

More and more, small grocery businesses were giving way to larger ones that were able to sell a wide range of foodstuffs under one roof, as well as provide adjacent parking which was becoming increasingly important. A real novelty was a self-service slot machine advertised by the Co-op as 'a 6-foot tall robot who serves night and day', which was installed in 1962. The range of products available included a large tin of Heinz baked beans at 1/2d, a medium tin of Nescafe for 2/4d, crisps for 4d, a large tin of Heinz vegetable soup for 10½d, a can of Pepsi for 3d and a 2lb bag of sugar for 2/3d – the automatic shop even gave change! Despite the growth of convenience food, virtually everybody who had a garden or allotment grew some kind of vegetables – even if it was only a row of runner beans. Those who had room also planted potatoes, peas, broad beans, carrots, onions and various members of the cabbage family. The more ambitious went in for lettuces, beetroot and leeks. Less common were fruit bushes, although there were blackcurrants, redcurrants, gooseberries and marrows if space allowed. Tomatoes were only found in greenhouses, which were uncommon, and no strawberries. We didn't even eat peppers, chillies or aubergines, let alone grow them.

Most villages held shows at which the competition between growers of fruit, flowers and vegetables was fierce and sometimes acrimonious with accusations of all kinds of malpractice. To manage to get an award in the domestic section of an agricultural show was the pinnacle of achievement, when even a 'Highly Commended' was something to boast about for the rest of the year. Classes included all types of the most popular fruit and vegetables, cakes, scones, jams, marmalade, honey, knitting, crochet and even home-made wine. For several weeks before the show, the prize of a shiny new spade was put on display in Hawkins' outfitters window.

Commercial television began in the UK in 1955 and brought about a radical change in how we saw food, even if it didn't alter our eating habits to the same extent. A large number (and arguably some of the best) of the early adverts were for food and drink, and had catchy jingles and slogans, some of which became catchphrases and most of which will be recalled by people of a certain age, in some cases decades after the products themselves had gone out of production.

There were considerable differences between what was supposed to be good for you then and now. Basically, the ideal was three square meals a day, the essential point being that they should be filling and preferably nourishing – how they tasted was not so important. The word 'nourishing' was in fact synonymous with calorific and, therefore, responsible for the wide expanses of puppy fat on view in the changing rooms of Britain. Meals were taken at mealtimes, which were more or less set in stone. Everyone had to 'come up to the table' and nobody ate from trays on their laps unless the house was exceptionally crowded. During the week breakfast in the home might include of some sort of egg, for these came in all guises, but principally boiled, scrambled or fried. The British Egg Marketing Board was responsible for one of the best-known and longest-surviving slogans, 'Go to Work on an Egg!' A version from the early 1950s featured cult comedian Tony Hancock. What is now known as the 'full English' was nowhere near as inclusive in the 1950s and '60s, and was generally saved for weekends and holiday times. Egg and bacon, sometimes with fried bread, was the usual cooked breakfast, but of course tomatoes, sausages, baked beans or mushrooms (but not all of these) might accompany them.

Sliced bread was well-established; Mother's Pride, which had first gone on sale in the north in 1936, was sold all over the country by 1956. Most sliced bread was white, while brown bread was represented by the slogan 'Don't just say brown, say Hovis'. If toasted, it might be covered by some sort of margarine such as Stork, although butter was still more popular. A lot of marmalade was made at home, normally from Seville oranges when they were in season, but 1lb jars of marmalade cost 1/2½d, or about 11p. There was a whole range of cereals to choose from, some of them, like Granola, Force and Kellogg's Corn Flakes, having been around since the beginning of the century. Bran Flakes (initially a cure for constipation) followed in 1915 and by the mid-1950s we were able to choose from a range which included Raisin Bran, Frosties, Rice Krispies ('Snap, Crackle and Pop'), Weetabix, Shredded Wheat, Quaker Oats and its speeded-up version, Ready Brek.

Tea bags had been around on a small scale since 1908 but didn't take off until the 1950s. This may well have been due, at least in part, to the Brooke Bond PG Tips adverts, which featured the Brooke Bond chimps in a whole range of situations. The first one, in 1956, showed boy and girl chimps dressed in Jane Austen-style costumes, drinking tea from elegant bone china cups. The voiceover was by Peter Sellers. Adverts like this showed that, far from being lazy, it was very stylish to use tea bags. Tea was much more popular than coffee, although the 'instants' were gaining ground. Posh people percolated their coffee and sometimes even ground their own beans. The delicious aroma of coffee being roasted was one of the attractions of 'high-class' grocers; the rest of us just put on the kettle and spooned Nescafe or Maxwell House into our mugs.

Children usually drank milk or squashes such as Kia-Ora (Maori for good health), Idris ('I drink Idris when I's dry, Idris is

the squash to buy') and Ribena, which at that time was always blackcurrant. Ribena was initially advertised as 'the blackcurrant health drink'. The runaway winner in regard to children's drink, though, was Corona, a carbonated and highly coloured drink which came in a range of (alleged) flavours. It was sold in large glass bottles with stoppers, which were removed and replaced by means of a wire cage that had to be eased on and off with the thumbs. Other fizzy drinks were Cola Cola and Pepsi Cola, and Tizer. Some mums produced home-made lemonade, but this was fiddly and expensive and didn't last long. It was also possible to buy packets of powder or crystals to make up with water, but although this was quick and easy, it tasted nothing like the real thing.

Families who had a shed, garage or spare room might make ginger beer. This involved the mixing of dried ginger, dried yeast, sugar and water to make a yeast culture known as a 'plant'. This had to be fed with ginger and sugar every day and was ready in about a week. The plant was then strained through muslin and lots more water and the juice from several lemons was added. Finally, the liquid was poured into 2-pint bottles and left to mature. The old plant had then to be divided: half put in fresh water to start another batch, the other thrown away or given to a friend or neighbour. This all sounds quite straightforward but there was quite an art to doing it successfully. Firstly, the correct amount of space had to be left between beer and bottle top in order to allow for expansion, otherwise explosions could, and did, occur. Secondly, it wasn't easy to judge when the beer was ready to drink; too soon and it would be weak and have no fizz, but if left too long it would become unpleasantly hot and slightly bitter. Mothers soon complained about the waste of ginger and sugar when half of it had to be thrown away (there were only so many people that you could give a new plant to).

Then there was the problem of having enough suitable bottles at hand when the time for making the next batch came round again. Potential explosions always sounded hilarious until you actually saw one, and if you had to help clear up the sticky mess it wasn't at all funny. One particularly bad series of eruptions resulted in a decorator being called in to repaint the living room ceiling and wash down the walls. Marital harmony was not restored for several days.

There was some confusion about what the midday meal should be called – for this was before the clear division of lunch being the one between morning and afternoon, and dinner the one in the evening. Both the names lunch hour and dinner hour were in use. To add to the confusion there was also 'high tea', which included something (often on toast) eaten with a knife and fork, and 'supper'.

Meat for a main meal was usually fresh (although prepacked meat had already put in an appearance) and was often ordered in advance from the butcher if it was for an important occasion. A joint of beef, pork or mutton was very much the centrepiece of Sunday dinner, although this meal could be eaten at any time between midday and late afternoon. This came with roast and/or mashed potatoes, and seasonal vegetables. 'All the trimmings' for beef consisted of a Yorkshire pudding put under the joint so that all the juices could run into it, and horseradish sauce and mustard sat ready on the table. Mutton, or lamb as it came to be, was served with mint sauce, and pork with apple sauce and sometimes stuffing.

A whole chicken was reserved for high days and holidays. These were often obtained from a nearby farm or smallholding and might arrive 'in feather'; so not only did the cook have to pluck them, they also had to 'draw' them, which meant removing all the internal organs that might still be warm and were invariably bloody. When the feet were chopped off, they might be given to children to play with as pulling the muscle and making the claws extend and contract was considered great fun. The chicken would be stuffed, traditionally with sage and onion, and served with bread sauce. Sausages might be used to make the meat go further, and if there were guests, chipolatas were looked on as more refined than the good old-fashioned banger.

To go with a family meal there were what were advertised as 'family drinks', like Whiteway's non-alcoholic Cydrax and Peardrax. Whatever meat was on the menu it was accompanied by satisfying gravy. For generations this had been made using the juices from the joint with flour carefully stirred into it until the correct thickness was obtained, but in the 1950s gravy powder (the long established 'Ah, Bisto!' goes back to the early part of the century) and then stock cubes took over. One of the most enduring television commercials was for Oxo, which gave meals 'man appeal'.

The traditional meal consisted of the famous 'meat and two veg'. Most of us were totally unaware of the concept of vegetarianism, let alone vegans, and very little concession was made to those who didn't eat meat. We never came across it at school, and if there had been any vegetarians among us they would doubtless have been labelled as 'faddy' and instructed to make do with whatever else was on offer.

Many old favourites now appear on the menus of restaurants and gastro pubs under the guise of traditional British fare, and are made with local organic ingredients, so bringing things round full circle. Among these, our everyday meals included: bangers and mash; corned beef 'ash; toad in the hole; chops, liver and onions with or without bacon; rissoles potatoes in their jackets; and just about anything fried or on toast. Most people's mums were expert in the making of pies and puddings containing steak and kidney, meat and potato, minced beef, cheese and onion, or fish. Stews and casseroles that 'stuck to your ribs' were warming and filling during the winter months, and wise caterers might keep a tin of something handy, such as Australian casserole steak at 2/3d a tin and the Co-op's own brand of canned peas or beans, which cost 10d (both the 1960 prices).

Some towns had shops which sold 'wet' fish (as opposed to fried) and which displayed their wares on marble slabs surrounded by ice, while other fishmongers came to the various markets with their wooden crates. Fish was relatively popular and many people continued the tradition of not eating meat on a Friday, although probably more from habit than for religious reasons. The cost-common fish were cod, haddock, sole, plaice and the different members of the herring family. A reasonably cheap meal could be made from smaller fish such as bloaters, or from roes on toast, while kippers were an alternative for breakfast.

If anyone didn't have time to cook, or for a special treat, there was always the chippy. Old photographs show 1960s menus and prices for fish and chips to take away from 1/9d:

Fish Cakes	6d
Fish Fillets	1/3d
Plaice	1/6d
Haddock	1/8d
Meat Burgers	10d
Steak and Kidney Pies	1/6d
Chicken and Chips	a hefty 3/6d

Inside, on the counter, gherkins and pickled eggs waited in enormous glass jars, and peas bubbled away in the saucepan.

In the north there were addition treats to be had, such as faggots and peas, potato scallops (*not* sea scallops) and mushy peas and gravy for the chips and pies. Some did home deliveries, but at this time all chippys closed on Mondays because there was no delivery of fresh fish on Sundays.

Salads (condemned as rabbit food) were not at all popular; hardly surprising in view of the fact that they consisted of little more than round lettuce leaves, slices of indigestible cucumber, quartered tomatoes, salad cream (mayonnaise being more unusual) and dressings almost unheard of. Cold meats, usually ham or corned beef, or grated cheese might be eaten with salad and the more adventurous added new potatoes and even coleslaw.

Sweet puddings and pies were made with fruit from your own or neighbours' gardens: apple, rhubarb, gooseberry and blackberries, when they were in season, could be gathered for free. Other favourites were crumbles, again usually made with apples, blackberry, rhubarb or gooseberries. Milk puddings were another cold-weather dish, the most common being rice. Although these could be bought for 1s a tin in the 1960s, they were usually home-made and served with a skin that you either loved or hated. One of our mothers still blushes when she remembers how efficient she felt when she made up a large rice pudding and put it carefully into the oven, ready to have a welcome hot meal when the family got back from visiting an agricultural show. All went well until she got back, went to take it from the oven and discovered the hard grains of rice still floating in cold milk as she had forgotten to light the oven before she left the house. Tins do have their uses. Other hot puds were bread and butter, the less interesting bread, suet and the universal sponge in all its many forms. Cream to go with any of these, or stewed or dried fruit which had to be pre-soaked over night, cost 1s for a 4oz tin. Even at our school, where there was an ongoing attempt to bring us up as young ladies, we had dinner rather than the more refined lunch, and ate it in the dinner hour.

We were provided with two courses at 1s a day, the weekly five bob to be collected first thing Monday morning by the form mistresses. Everyone in our year handed over their money personally every week. Although school dinners for those from needy families were paid for by the local authority, we never saw any evidence of this. There were no packed lunches and only one girl went home to dinner, even amongst the local girls who came to school on their bikes. What we had for school dinners in the 1950s and '60s was very similar to what was being wolfed down in similar institutions all over the country, and indeed had been for years before this. There were stews and pies and the occasional suet pudding, but it's hard to remember let alone identify what type of meat they contained. Everything was served in oblong metal containers resembling army billycans and these became extremely hot, so that the kitchen ladies treated them with caution and handled them with tea towels. Vegetables were cabbage, carrots, potatoes and swede, all boiled to within an inch of their lives.

The one exception to the non-descript first courses was the superb cottage pie, which had well-flavoured minced beef topped with deliciously crispy mashed potato. Every scrap of this was scraped from round the container, competition being fierce for this honour. The amount that each container held was noticeably different and on one never-to-be-forgotten day someone on our table noticed on the way into the dining room that there was an extra full one a couple of tables away. As we were the first people to arrive, she decided to swap that tin with ours, and subsequently went across to grab it. She'd forgotten how hot they were, however, and gave a shriek and dropped it on to the parquet flooring of the hall. Of course we had to sacrifice our own tin and make do with what hadn't ended up on the floor. We watched the depressing sight of our friend vainly trying to sweep the steaming heap into a dustpan while her own much depleted helping congealed on the plate. In the summer a rather unusual salad would appear, attractively arranged in colourful rows of pilchards, grated carrot, dates, beetroot and cucumber, all served with mashed potato.

Winter puddings were a range of sponges (aka stodges): plain with golden syrup and yellow custard; pink with colour co-ordinated custard; chocolate with chocolate sauce; and sometimes a spotted dick or crumble, just for a change. In summer we had dried fruit, prunes, apricots and apple rings – re-hydrated with varying degrees of success – and served with, yes, custard. We also had jelly and custard, by which it will be seen that we floated on oceans of the stuff. An all-year-rounder was the despised semolina, which came lukewarm and runny with optional dollop of cheap jam. Once, and only once, we had the most heavenly chocolate tart, so good that we went to the kitchen to ask if there was any leftover. Later, when we asked if we could have the tart again, we were told it was too expensive.

At one school:

Meals were made on the premises and were good, apart from the semolina! Looking back now they were well balanced e.g. if we had meat pie there was always fruit for pudding. The jam roly-poly and custard was to die for! Don't ever remember having chips but we did have salad. We were encouraged to sit with pupils of other ages and mix. There were two sixth-formers on each table to keep order and a weekly rota for servers. Every pupil was on it.

Not everyone appreciated all the food though, as this anec-
dote shows:

> K hated fish and usually, after explaining this, she was
> allowed to leave it. On one particular day we had Miss T
> on dinner duty. She had ginger hair and a temper to match.
> She insisted that K must eat the fish as she believed her
> dislike of it was all in the mind! K kept refusing and saying
> that she would be sick. The whole table of eight of us were
> kept sitting there until K ate the fish, which she did even-
> tually after about an hour because we were all moaning
> at her. Miss T stood at the end of the table looking smug
> until K stood up and promptly threw up all over Miss T's
> feet and new shoes. K was sent home. Needless to say her
> parents didn't complain or threaten to sue as they would
> today. [Neither, it should be added, did Miss T.!]

Other memories evoked by the mention of school dinners
are of:

> … shepherd's pie, pastry topped meat pies, sausages,
> fish on Fridays. Veg such as carrots or cabbage, potatoes
> mashed, roasted or boiled. Gravy. Puddings were mainly
> 'stodge', (e.g. spotted dick and custard or ginger pudding
> with cornflour sauce) or fruit pie and custard. Table moni-
> tors (girls sitting at the end of the table) cut up and served
> out the helpings.

> You ate what you were given, because that's what you did
> then. Fudge tart was wonderful and winter salad was awful.

> Can't remember much about them although I always liked
> school custard.

I honestly don't know what was in Dinosaur Stew. I doubt that there was much meat, and I suspect that it might have been scrag end of something! The name was one of many that had been handed down through successive generations of pupil diners. To dine in the Refectory, and sit on the long benches, under the portraits of John Hampden et al, was presumably a preparation for Oxbridge. I can still taste the polish! I can also remember the prune-eating competition, and the dire effect on the winner (a second year pupil from Long Crendon). Spam fritters were gorgeous.

This latter description of what was served up to our male counterparts shows just how traditional school meals could be.

What we had to eat when we got home depended on our parents' midday arrangements. Some of us had a further full meal, whereas others had high tea or tea and supper. Baked beans, spaghetti, sardines, egg or cheese on toast, or a sandwich, cake and a hot drink; the combinations were many. Many households made jam from their own or donated fruit, but strawberry jam was frequently bought readymade at about 1/8d for a 1lb jar due to the problems with setting and the seasonality of strawberries.

Apart from milk and a biscuit for 'elevenses', a hot drink like Horlicks, Ovaltine or Bournvita and another biscuit before they went off to bed, children were rarely given food between meals. If you didn't eat at the 'proper' time (that is, one that suited your parents), you went without. Snacks were reserved for times when you were out and about and couldn't have a 'proper' meal, rather than used as food supplements. The first flavoured crisps I remember were chicken ones, introduced in 1961, but the unsalted type with the blue twist of salt lasted long afterwards. It was also possible to buy cheap bags of broken crisps, although these were much less common than broken biscuits.

The only concession that was made to eating between meals was the large tray of buns sent up by the bakery in the village. These arrived at school shortly before the mid-morning break and were delivered into the hands of two, supposedly responsible, members of the class who even at that early age had learnt the art of insider trading and managed to bag what they and their friends wanted before the tray was offered to hoi polloi. The reason for the urgency to gain access to the buns was the fact that there were three types: the highly desirable cream ones which cost 3*d*; the second-best 2*d* iced fingers, which despite invariably being a bit stale were still popular; and the common or garden-plain ones, which cost 1*d*. In any case, there were never enough buns for all the hopeful purchases.

Needless to say, sweetshops were a great attraction. Sweet rationing, which had started in 1942 and finished in February 1953, had little effect on us. There were several sweetshops in our town, some of them were tobacconists and newsagents as well, but there were two old-fashioned little shops that only sold sweets and one was a magnet for the town's children. Unfortunately, the spinster who owned the second one was mentally unstable and tended to chase customers away rather than welcome them. She would dart out of the shop and hurl abuse at passers-by, many of whom were pillars of the little community. She used to run behind the dustcart, which at that time was open and pulled by a shire horse, and shake her duster into it. One well-meaning mother went into the shop to give the unfortunate woman her custom, but found that the sweets were stuck together in lumps and the chocolate stale. Even if it had been edible, there were no paper bags to put it in. The shopkeeper became more and more eccentric and eventually the shop closed.

The successful shop was on the ground floor of an ancient building and looked like something from the pages of a Dickens novel. The interior was dark with one wall filled with boxes of all the rubbishy confectionery so beloved by children. There were Black Jacks, Fruit Salads, flying saucers, sherbet fountains and Dib Dabs, gobstoppers, sweet cigarettes and all manner of liquorice novelties: pipes, bootlaces, Allsorts, Catherine wheels and Pontefract cakes. Behind the counter was shelf upon shelf of glass bottles with screw tops and these held acid drops, Everton Mints, all sorts of toffees, peanut brittle, aniseed balls, pear drops, clove balls, winter mixture, honeycomb, Bull's Eyes, humbugs, fudge, barley sugar, butterscotch, rhubarb and custard, Parma Violets, Love Hearts and much, much more. Lurking in the middle of it all was the proprietor, an elderly widow dressed in a Hilda Ogden-style turban and wraparound overall, waiting with ill-concealed impatience as we tried to decide what was the best value for our money.

More respectable confectionery which was enjoyed by everybody included Murray Mints (the 'too-good-to-hurry mints, Why make haste when you can taste the hint of mint in Murray Mints?'), Black Magic and Dairy Box chocolates and Polo Mints ('the Mint with a Hole') from the Rowntree factory. This firm used the well-known slogan 'Don't forget the Fruit Gums, Mum!', which dates from 1956 but was forcibly altered on account of what was termed 'unfair pressure on mums'. The later version was 'don't forget the fruit gums, chum'. In addition to the classic Dairy Milk (the bars of which ranged from the 1d one in silver paper to the largest in the famous purple wrapper), big names from Cadbury were Picnic, Creme Egg, Milk Tray, Flake and Crunchie, and from Mars were Maltesers, Bounty and, of course, Mars Bars, from Nestlé came Milkybar and the relaunched Milky Way. Fry's offered Five Boys and Chocolate and Peppermint Cream bars, but it's for the legendary Turkish Delight advert that it's best remembered. It was set among desert sand dunes and showed an exotic girl slave, complete with yashmak, being unrolled from an oriental carpet in front of a sheik. She proceeded to feed him chunks of Fry's Turkish Delight, which, the voiceover whispered seductively, was 'full of Eastern promise'. Then there were the round, flat Clarnico Mints with their delicious melting centres, and Newberry Fruits, crystallised orange and lemon slices and so very many more.

As for chewing gum, you didn't even need to go into a shop as you could get a square pack of Beechnut with the crisp, strong, minty coating from a machine out in the street if you had two penny pieces handy. We always started off to Guide meetings with these coins at the ready (it wasn't just Scouts who had to be prepared), for if we ever needed to make calls from a public phone box. Having produced them for inspection, we'd inevitably put them into the chewing-gum machine as soon as we got the chance.

Women seldom went into pubs and never alone. There were men-only bars and even a few men-only pubs. The average pub was smoky, often smelling of stale beer and with little to attract women or families unless there was a dining room or family area. Popular with ladies who *were* taken into respectable pubs were ladylike drinks such as Dubonnet, Snowballs and Babycham ('I'd lurv a Babycham'). This is sparkling perry, which is still available today, with a trademark little yellow deer, a plastic model of which graced many a bar. We didn't accompany our parents into pubs but were parked outside with fizzy lemonade and a packet of crisps. Unknown to them, however, at the age of 14 or so we used to go into a local pub (which shall remain nameless), where the bar staff cheerfully served us with lagers and lime or the cheaper light and lime, no questions asked.

At home we were entertained by the TV and the adverts, such as the one showing cartoon yokels singing 'Coates comes up from Somerset, where the cider apples grow!' and the one for Mackeson brown ale, which we heard 'looks good, tastes good and, by golly, it does you good'. There was also: 'Mann's brown is the best brown ale, best brown ale, best brown ale, Mann's brown is the best brown ale, drink some today' or 'Guinness is good for you, so think what two can do' – the toucan remains the Guinness mascot to this day.

Even though business people might eat at pubs and hotels, the rest of us hardly every did apart from on birthdays, anniversaries and special occasions like passing exams. At the top of the tree were the very expensive restaurants to be found in town-centre hotels, none of which we were likely ever to set foot in. Top-class restaurants arranged dinner dances, while establishments which advertised themselves as 'grills' were also popular for a civilised night out as they were seen as chic. In market towns like ours, hotels had their own dining rooms which were open to non-residents. Then there were the quaint eateries of the Olde Thatch variety (unlicensed, open 10 a.m. to 8 p.m.) where lunch could be had for 9/6*d* to 11/6*d* and tea at 4/6*d*. At the more expensive ones, lunch cost from 12/6*d* and dinner from 15/-. The more enterprising pub landlords had begun to offer food in the 1950s but the progression from packets of crisps and peanuts to the basic pork pies, sandwiches and sausage rolls, and then on to soup and ploughman's lunches and finally trendy foreign dishes, took several years.

The nearest we ourselves got to eating out was to haunt the town's newly opened, one and only coffee bar. In there we were able to try all sorts of new delights, such as frothy coffee and milkshakes. The eating side of things was confined to packets of crisps and Penguin bars, but who cared? Another big attraction was the juke box; the first one that we'd ever come across. This cost as much as the drinks did, but as the cafe was patronised by dashing young delivery men, drivers and builders who had money to spend on such things, we were usually able to persuade them to play our favourites.

Nine

Don't it Make you Feel Good?, The Shadows, 1964

By no means did all houses have inside toilets; some had no baths, let alone showers. After the return of men to their families at the end of the war and the resultant 'baby boom', some people didn't even have a home. Homelessness was a real problem, even in our prosperous part of the country, and the homeless families' unit in Oxford was reported full in 1963. The year that we started grammar school a new set of public baths, consisting of six baths and four showers, was opened in Oxford. Adults were charged 6*d* (and OAPs 4*d*) for a slipper bath and 4*d* for a shower, while towels cost 3*d* and soap a penny. Most, but not all, of those in my class lived in houses with indoor toilets and bathrooms, although some of us had family and friends who had to go into the back yard when they needed the toilet (using a chamber pot in the night) and taking their turn to wash in the sink in the kitchen.

Despite the fact that bathing or showering could be something of a challenge, more and more brands of soap and other toiletries appeared in the 1950s and '60s. The majority of them were launched to the accompaniment of memorable jingles on the newly opened commercial television. Old-established soaps were Knight's Castile (we couldn't understand why it wasn't 'Castle'), Imperial Leather (not 'Lather'? Its slogan was 'Rare but good') and Palmolive ('milder with olive oil, smoother with olive oil, gentlest soap of all'). 'Cadum for Madam' was the slogan of a toilet soap introduced into the UK by Colgate-Palmolive in 1955 from France, where it had been popular since 1907. Some other less glamorous old faithfuls had been around for generations, such as Wright's Coal Tar, Pear's and even carbolic.

In the 1950s Lux was billed as 'the soap of the stars!' and an early 1960s advert had pop star Sandie Shaw confiding:

> I asked if I could sing about Lux but they said: no, just use your own words. Well, I think New Lux is fantastic, and really new! It's got a new wrapper and a wonderful new perfume – just the kind I go for! But what's really marvellous about New Lux is the new silky lather! It seems more than just a lather, it feels like a rich cream, and leaves my complexion so soft and smooth! New Lux makes me feel really good all over … right down to my toes! Try it yourself – see how great it is!

So there. When Camay was launched in the UK in 1958, it was with the jingle 'You'll look a little lovelier each day, with fabulous pink Camay', a claim that would probably attract the attentions of trades description officials nowadays. The deodorant soap Lifebuoy appeared in 1962 as an antidote to the dreaded BO:

> Living at today's non-stop pace, it's harder than ever to stay fresh.
> So say NO to BO with new Lifebuoy toilet soap –
> Now more effective against BO than ever!

The Lifebuoy advertisement's pressure not to be an unconscious stinker was relentless, and its campaign continued with a sinister voice whispering in the victim's ear, 'BO, your best friend won't tell you'.

Bath time, for those that had baths, could be enlivened by throwing in handful of lurid-coloured bath salts or crumbling a bath cube into the running water. The adventurous could experiment with bath foam as well, but many mums just added a few drops of a disinfectant such as Dettol. As well as bath night, Friday was hair-washing night. As the advert for Amami setting lotion said, 'Friday night is Amami night'. Many of today's shampoos, such as Silvikrin, Pantene and Head & Shoulders, were around then, plus Gloria, Halo and Dreen which have since disappeared. There were home perm kits from Toni ('Which twin has the Toni?'), Twink and Richard Hudnut, among others.

The very first advert shown on commercial television in Britain on 22 September 1955 came with the jingle 'It's tingling fresh, It's fresh as ice. It's Gibbs SR toothpaste'. Its predecessor, Gibbs Dentifrice, a sort of compressed powder, came in flat tins with a picture of 'ivory towers' (teeth, not tusks) on the lid. One of the best adverts and jingles went:

> *You'll wonder where the yellow went*
> *When you brush your teeth with Pepsodent.*

For whiter teeth, fresher breath … Pepsodent!
You'll wonder where the yellow went
When you go steady with Pepsodent!

There was also 'Maclean's white teeth mean healthy teeth, but half-clean teeth are not', followed by 'Have you Macleaned your teeth today? Have, you? We did!' In 1959 Crest toothpaste pandered to the fear of visits to the dentist with 'Look mum, no cavities!'

Very few people bought deodorants or antiperspirants, although you could get the sticky, smelling Mum lotion in a lilac-coloured plastic squeezy bottle (pre-aerosols, but roll-ons were available), regular applications of soap and water being considered quite adequate. There were of course soaps which contained deodorants but these could irritate and cause rashes.

In our youth, one of the less pleasant aspects of personal hygiene was the hard, shiny toilet rolls and folded sheets, which smelt of disinfectant and had macho names like Bronco and Izal. It's small wonder that people risked blocking up their toilets with any tissue paper that came to hand and the traditional squares of torn-up newspaper, which survived in outside loos. Nobody used paper handkerchiefs; instead of the now-universal tissue, there were cotton hankies: giant ones like table cloths for men, or a really bad cold, and dainty, semi-transparent wisps for ladies. There was even quite a selection for children too, with fairies, flowers and nursery rhyme characters on them. All of these had to be boiled to keep them hygienic and a respectable colour. Similarly, there were no disposable nappies, these being made of terry cotton which had to be soaked and then boiled.

Most of us started our periods before or during our first year at secondary school, but we weren't sure who had or hadn't as this was still very much a taboo subject. A close friend might say 'Do you use sanitary towels yet?' or something equally tactful. By the time we got to the third year we were a bit more blasé about it, but it still wasn't a topic for general conversation. We usually referred to it as coming or being 'on'. We sometimes called it 'the curse' but we were aware of the various contemporary names for a period – time of the month, monthlies, courses, red flag (leakages), red-letter days, woman thing, tummy troubles, flowers. We all used sanitary towels (abbreviated to STs), which were attached by loops to an elastic sanitary belt. Although tampons had been on the market for decades we never came across anyone who used them. They were objected to on the belief that they did away with your virginity by breaking the hymen and, even worse, they could 'get lost' by making their way up the vagina and into the womb, never to be seen again.

There was an unending difficulty about what to do if you came on during school hours. For the first year or so our periods tended to be irregular, so it meant a choice between carrying bulky towels around on the off chance and risking them being spotted when you were taking books and writing things out of your school bag, or getting caught out. There were no vending machines in the school toilets and we'd have been embarrassed at asking a friend to help out. Maybe we could have got towels from the school office, but none of us would have thought to go there let alone pluck up courage to ask the school secretary such a personal thing. Usually we made do with padding our knickers with yards of loo paper every hour or so, and hoping for the best.

Then there was the problem of disposal. Our mothers impressed upon us the fact that we were very lucky not to have to put soiled terry towels (successors to the traditional rags) in a bucket to soak overnight and then wash them and get them dried for the next month, in secret of course. It was difficult to change towels at school as there were no paper bags and bins to leave them in, let alone incinerators in which to burn them. Going out with friends, or worse, on a date, during your period was a potential nightmare. If we were unable to change them, the towels chafed the tender skin of the inner thigh unbearably. Getting used towels home safely wasn't the end of the ordeal for they had to be burnt in a fire-place or dustbin, discreetly and away from inquisitive eyes. Whoever wrote 'I Enjoy Being a Girl' couldn't have been one!

Every home had its medicine cabinet containing an assortment of items from the tried and tested to the newly advertised miracle cure. Newspapers of the time car-ried advertisements, which look very old-fashioned to the modern eye and reminiscent of quack remedies, although the majority were nothing of the kind and were probably a good deal safer than today's chemical concoctions. The condition 'exhaustipation', invented specifically for a Carter's Little Liver Pills newspaper advert in the mid-1950s, must have been pounced on eagerly by any aspiring hypochondriacs who were looking to add a new ailment to their portfolios. Symptoms included waking up in the morning 'feeling tired, sour and headachy'. The cause was a troubled colon, and of course the pills were more than up for the job.

Aspro, the brand name for a type of aspirin, came in sickly pink packets whereas common or garden aspirins were sold in box-less paper strings. Aspirin was used as a pain reliever for just about anything from arthritis to period pains. Beecham's Powders, which contain aspirin and caffeine, were also popu-lar painkillers. However, these long-standing items were being challenged by new products with their modern advertise-ments, like 'Phensic is better for headaches than Aspirin alone'.

Cough mixture (or syrup or linctus) was another must. Older brands like Buttercup cough syrup and Galloways had to compete with Veno's and its superb advertisement featuring a singing snowman, who informed us:

I'm the Veno's snowman, call me Pop,
You'll find me in the chemist's shop.

Chests and throats might benefit from the strongly smelling wintergreen ointment and Vick, which came in fat little jars, could be rubbed in, used to make a vapour to inhale, or put in the mouth to dissolve. Sufferers from blocked-up noses and sinuses would put a few drops of sticky brown friar's balsam into a bowl of boiling water, disappear under a towel and inhale the fumes until the water got cold.

In the days before adequate health-and-safety measures were in force, a first-aid kit was essential. For patching up cuts in the kitchen and playground there was a pack of fabric sticking plaster, not yet waterproof and in a roll so that you had to cut off what was needed. Iodine was dabbed on to little soldiers who'd been in the wars, and stung more than the wound itself. Bright pink Germolene ointment was also applied to cuts and grazes, as was the nauseous smelling, mildly antiseptic TCP, which doubled up as a liquid to gargle when diluted. Eyes were bathed with lotion or eyewash poured into a blue glass eyebath from a bottle of Optrex.

For those who had overdone the eating and drinking or gobbled up their food too quickly there were plenty of remedies. Livers might be 'woken up' with Calomel, a potentially dangerous remedy which had been used by the Victorians to treat cholera cases. Epsom Salts, too, have been around for generations, but they had competition from Andrews Liver Salts with their jingle 'Andrews, Andrews for inner cleanliness' – for nobody wanted a dirty inside:

Eno's Fruit Salts
E-N-O, Eno!
When you're feeling low, Eno!
It's mild and gentle, and good tasting too
E-N-O, Eno!

These all fizzed in the most exciting way when put in water and we loved watching this happen, even if they weren't all that easy to get down. Easier to swallow were Milk of Magnesia in its blue glass bottle and the more portable tablets, Rennies and Settlers, which brought 'express relief'. Luckily we had little need of this relief, but constipation sometimes struck even the healthiest of us. When this happened our mums would bring out the California Syrup of Figs, which was over-sweet but not objectionable, or the disgusting liquid paraffin, which was slimy and tasted of nothing.

Members of the older generation were asked if they were 'Losing vitality? Feeling low? Run down?' If the answer was yes, luckily 'A course of Sanatogen restores your health'. If it didn't there was always Phyllosan, a supplement which, we were assured, 'fortifies the over-40s'. For those who preferred liquid relief, a bottle of Wincarnis tonic wine might be kept in the drinks cabinet.

Health care for us at school was very low key. There was a remedial exercise class in the gym, last period on Monday afternoons, for the flat footed, the asthmatic and other lame ducks. We seem to have been the only school that wasn't visited by the 'nit nurse', although a nurse did come to give us injections from time to time. We'd had polio and other vaccinations when very young. If, when out with us in our prams, our mothers came across another mother pushing a bawling red-faced infant anywhere near the Baby Welfare Clinic, she would ask if there were any inoculations to be had just as eagerly as she'd enquired about the possibility of getting sausages a few years earlier. When word got round, every self-respecting mother would rush her offspring round to the clinic and get them 'done'. Similarly, just about everybody had already had measles, mumps, whooping cough and, much less frequently, scarlet fever. If either of our parents heard of children that they knew having caught an infectious disease, we were packed off to play with them in order to catch it and get it over with. This was considered of particular importance when it concerned little boys getting mumps.

We had to have a course of anti-tetanus injections because some sheep had been making merry in the grounds during the holidays. Another was the BCG vaccination against TB. As one pupil recalls:

> When I was at Grammar School I remember the polio vaccine – on a spoon – and the TB jab. I remember sniffing at something really hard and had to be taken to lie down as I almost fainted. It may have been the stuff that's put on your arm before the jab. I seem to recall someone having their arm scratched with a needle but cannot remember anything else about it.

This would have been due to a smallpox scare in 1962 when there was mass immunisation in the UK. We were all incredibly brave when compared with the stories we'd heard about soldiers allegedly being lined up for jabs and falling down in a faint like ninepins before they were anywhere near the needle.

We may have had visits from a school dentist, as pupils did elsewhere, but if we did they must have been very low key and not caused the terror which they inspired in other places. Visits to dentists generally were very unpleasant; the needles which gave the anaesthetic seemed as big as knitting needles and the drill made as much noise as those used in road works. Although it didn't hurt, the 'gas' used for a full anaesthetic when you were having a tooth out made some people sick, and everyone was woozy for some time afterwards.

If we were taken ill at school it was impossible to go home early. We were about a mile away from public transport and there was no question of mothers coming to the school to collect poorly offspring. One of the reasons for this that most homes didn't have a phone, the other that mothers didn't have access to a car as they do today. We just had to make the best of it until we could be bundled on and off the bus and stagger through our front door at the usual time. Fortunately, the usual afflictions were painful periods, bad colds and, during our first year, an outbreak of flu. Sufferers, once they were proved to be genuine, would be wrapped up in large blankets, with a hot water bottle if appropriate, and put out in the relative peace and quiet of the front porch on a put-me-up kept especially for this purpose. They might be visited by a select number of friends (no more than two at the bedside at once), who approached the patient with due respect and promised to make sure that she reached home safely.

We were only one generation away from the folk medicine concocted by wise women but it was too soon for the revival of herbal remedies. An aunt managed to get the warts on her hand 'charmed away' by giving a woman she knew for 6d. Never mind how, but they went. Another cure for warts was to rub a piece of raw meat over them then bury the meat and as it rotted the wart disappeared. We were never fed the 'sure-fire remedy' of fried mice for whooping cough, but we did have boiled onions whopped on to boils to bring the poison out, and very painful it was too.

If the worst came to the worst and a visit to the doctor's surgery became unavoidable, it was not a particularly pleasant experience – although more personal and a good deal less time-consuming than a trip to a hospital or health centre today. Doctors practised in separate surgeries, which were often part of their own homes, and sometimes there were joint practices but no health centres at this time. GPs would diagnose, dispense medication and perform minor operations, in addition to which they were on call round the clock. There were cottage hospitals (community hospitals) in the smaller towns but for anything serious we were referred to hospitals in the larger towns and cities. Luckily, very few of us were referred to hospital apart from the few unfortunates who broke bones which had to be put in plaster, and even they got some satisfaction in collecting signatures on their 'pots'.

Ten

Hooray! Hooray! It's a Holi-Holiday, Boney M, 1979

In England, New Year's Day wasn't a public holiday until 1974, so once Christmas and Boxing Day were over there was nothing for us to look forward to until the Easter break. Some Scottish people celebrated Hogmanay and went first-footing, but we contented ourselves by waiting for Big Ben to strike twelve o'clock and then watching the celebrations of those who did see the New Year in, broadcast from Edinburgh and London. There were dances such as the Chelsea Arts Ball and in central London revellers jumped into the fountains in Trafalgar Square.

Apart from the religious services, Easter wasn't a huge festival and we only had a week or so off then. Everyone had hot cross buns and children were all given chocolate Easter eggs, or sometimes cardboard ones with a small gift inside.

In the bigger towns, confectioners would possibly have a giant chocolate egg on display at the front of their windows. Decorated all over with brightly coloured sugar flowers and piped icing designs, these eggs were destined to be taken off to children's homes and be enjoyed there.

In total we had six weeks off school in the summer, plus two days for each half term and about a week for Christmas and Easter. It wouldn't have crossed anyone's mind to arrange a family holiday during term time, as people do today without a second thought. This might have had something to do with the fact that most people still stayed in Britain, where the season was very much defined by the weather. There was no incentive, therefore, to go away for cheaper breaks during term. Another reason was the fact that some workplaces, such as factories, had set weeks off in the summer which all the employees took off at the same time.

At other schools local visits were almost non-existent, so in that aspect we were lucky, even though it wouldn't have appeared so to the casual observer. Apart from the unfortunate trips to the Old Vic and the county show, we were taken to several other places of interest locally, including seeing a production of *Romeo and Juliet* at the theatre. This made so much of an impression on us that a couple of bold souls wrote fan letters to the actor who played Romeo but, not surprisingly, didn't get a reply. By sheer coincidence, we were to have this play on our O level English literature syllabus.

At the end of the fourth year we had re-established our reputations sufficiently well to be taken on another outing, although this time it was a less ambitious one and confined within the county boundaries. The theme was local history/heritage and there was to be little scope for misbehaving – in any case two teachers were sent with us. In the event, we were all feeling very mellow after the success of the school

fete the previous day and the prospect of weeks of summer holidays which lay ahead. A day out was itself a sort of mini-holiday to us. It should be remembered that in those days there were no motorways in Oxfordshire and few towns had bypasses, so the pace was leisurely along what were virtually country lanes and through market towns and small villages.

The attitude towards jaunts away from school of the school where the pupil had had the worst experience was probably to be expected: 'I don't think we ever had a visit anywhere. It was made clear to us from the start that school was where we worked all the time, and home was where we worked most of the time.' Similarly, there were no trips from three of the other schools and none that were remembered from a further five. Someone else said they too hadn't been on any 'except to the local baths, but we did do work experience'. Those that did go somewhere didn't go far or frequently: 'Apart from a trip to the House of Commons in the sixth form, and a few to the theatre, I don't think we went any-where.' Male outings were limited to 'Colin Quartly's farm [a couple of miles down the road] in 1st year Geography and Huntley & Palmers (Biscuits) in Reading, London, Oxford, et cetera'. In another school: 'we went to visit a sewage works, probably after exams. I think we went on another trip – I have a class photo somewhere but I can't remember where we went.' The 'archaeological digs around the town and other local history walks including the parish church' sound more promising, as do 'Petworth House and nature trips to the Downs nearby'. At one grammar school, visits were not memorable apart from 'Sixth-form visits to art galleries such as Port Sunlight and to Stratford to see *Henry V*. Field-study trips to Hythe in Kent and to Scotland.'

During the long summer break virtually everyone went to the seaside, not to historic places or beauty spots such as the

Lakes or the Yorkshire Dales. Normally holidays lasted only a week and destinations were reached by coach or train. Sometimes coach trips were arranged, the cost of which could be paid off a little at a time throughout the year. These were especially popular as the essentials were paid for in advance so everyone knew how much spending money they had got to play with. Also, there was always plenty of company and we could bring all our buys home in the boot of the coach. Nobody near us went to a holiday camp, although of course everyone had heard of Butlins and Pontins. Camping and caravanning were beginning to take off but by far the most common form of accommodation was the seaside boarding house, the forerunner of today's guest house. Many of us had personal experiences of boarding houses, especially at Blackpool. From the 1940s to the '60s a local man organised two trips a year to Blackpool, once in the summer and again when the Illuminations were on in the early autumn.

The facilities offered by this type of accommodation were limited to say the least. Rooms held two or three beds, some doubles, some twins and, if necessary, a cot could be squeezed in as well so that all the family could be together in one room. They certainly weren't designed to be used for anything apart from sleeping as there was no room for desks or easy chairs, let alone televisions, hospitality trays or ensuites. There was a chilly bare bathroom on most, but not all, floors and a limited number of separate unisex toilets with high cisterns and chains. These days, when virtually all accommodation is en suite, it's difficult to imagine the trials of sharing a toilet (which may or may not have been in a bathroom) with a houseful of strangers. Anyone going to the loo after they had changed into their night clothes would put on a coat or mac, poke their heads round the bedroom door and if the coast was clear, scuttle along the corridor and maybe up or down a few steps to reach the loo. If they were unlucky it might already be occupied, if not they might be disturbed by urgent rattling of the door handle as someone else tried their luck. We were always too tired and excited to sleep through that first night but it didn't matter a bit as we knew that in the morning we'd get up to the glorious smell of bacon escaping from the kitchen and making its way up the stairs. Why does it always smell so much more tempting than it actually tastes? It was possible to have a (limited) number of things for breakfast, from just toast or cereal to various fried items.

That first saunter along the front in the daylight was the best one of the week. We would inspect the new attractions and make sure that our old favourites were still around. The smell of the donkeys and the leather of their tack; the 7 miles of beach; the kiosks selling hot dogs, candy floss, ice creams, beach balls, buckets and spades. We went to our special chippy most days as the midday meal wasn't included and returning to the boarding house during the day was discouraged at most places, if not actually forbidden. A few places still included a midday meal but this was gradually being phased out as people bought sandwiches or something from the chippy, or went out for the day and had a meal elsewhere.

On our way back in the late afternoon, we'd peer into the dining rooms of other guest houses that we passed and see what we thought of their decor and the way the tables were set out. One member of our coach load took exception to sauce bottles being left out on the tables, but another was adamant that this was a good thing as it saved guests having to ask every time they wanted sauce. What put everybody off, we were all agreed, was limp lettuce with half a tomato and a slice of plastic meat, all of which had been put out well in advance of high-tea time and was well past its prime by the time the guests came into the dining room. The sauce and salad cream bottles were certainly an indicator of what was served up at mealtimes in boarding houses in the 1950s and '60s. The dishes that appeared were limited in scope and people who'd been before or who were in their second week knew just what to expect, although not necessarily the order in which they would put in an appearance.

Boarding houses were generally unlicensed and anyone who wanted a drink had to go out to a pub or club. There would be a lounge where residents could gather to smoke and chat against the background of the television, which was left on all the time. About 9 p.m. the landlord would come round with a hot drink and a couple of biscuits for those to whom bed was singing its irresistible siren song. The front door would be locked about an hour later, although anyone going out to a late-finishing show could use the Yale key, which shared a key ring with the one to their room. Occasionally there wasn't even an indoor toilet and fond memories of 1960s holidays include having to grab a stick and rush to the rescue of a mother besieged in a Welsh privy by a flock of angry geese. Another treat was being provided with a jug, washbasin and chamber pot in an elderly widow's house where the only water was in the kitchen and the loo outside in the yard.

To return to the subject of camping, for many of us Girl Guide camps were a feature of our junior years. Our first experience of the mixed pleasures of sleeping under canvas was when we went off to stay on land belonging to the county commissioner, miles from anywhere. We'd practised knots, lashing the ends of ropes and all the other skills that came under the heading of 'camp craft', and now was the time to do them for real. One of the first things was to construct a triangle of sticks to support washing bowls, but possibly the most important chore was to dig out the latrines and put a hessian barricade round them. We had to set to and pitch our own tents, not huge affairs but big enough to hold about four of us in each. Corners were chosen and sleeping bags settled in each. As it was summer, we had our blue dresses rather than the full uniform and we'd been allowed to bring along shorts and bathing costumes. One of us had changed into her costume, a flesh-coloured little one-piece, for an hour's sun-bathing when the commissioner spotted her and shouted to her in no uncertain terms to go and put her clothes on.

During the time that we were in camp we had to rely on cooking over an open fire, which had to be lit and carefully doused each day. The menu was uninspired and certainly unbalanced – the predictable jacket potatoes, sausages and dampers – but whatever it was it was eagerly awaited and the proud cooks congratulated. By no means was all day spent in camp; we were taken on outings, notably a steamer trip on the Thames, where the slow pace and waiting about in locks drove us to distraction, and to Chessington Zoo, which was much more to our liking. What made things even more fun was the fact that several of our friends from another company were camping close by and we were able to join them for outings and sing-songs round the camp fire.

Some people's parents took them abroad, but not just to sit around on the beach. The aim was either cultural, Italy or Greece, or to admire scenery, Austria or Switzerland. Package holidays were in their infancy and although there were already some to Spanish and Italian resorts to soak up the sun and even a little foreign culture, they were very much family affairs with no hint of bars or clubbing of any kind. It was possible to get very reasonable holidays for a few days to discover the delights of Paris, the Dutch bulb fields or even the Norwegian fjords, all of which cost under £20 each.

Apart from family holidays to the sea there were day trips, again usually to the coast (the nearest to us being Southsea, but also to Bognor and Bournemouth). Weymouth was that bit further and occasionally we even went as far as the Isle of Wight or Southend, which were reached by boat on the Thames from London. Many of these were choir outings, although clubs and pubs ran them as well. While spending any time at one of the larger seaside resorts it was a good idea to keep your eyes open for a representative from one of the more popular daily newspapers (the most likely were the *Daily Mail*, *Daily Express*, *Daily Mirror* and the *Daily Sketch*) who might be patrolling the proms and piers, waiting for a reader daring enough to challenge him, brandish a copy of the correct paper and claim a cash prize. This was not as easy as it sounds for these young men looked very much the same as the hundreds of other holiday-makers strolling along with a newspaper under his arm. Of course it had to be the right paper, and how embarrassing would it be to accost the wrong person! Just as bad would be to identify Mr or Miss X while still on your way to buy the paper, or to miss out as he handed over the cash to a bold someone a few deckchairs along from where you were sitting.

Fish 'n' chips, bread and butter and a pot of tea or a glass of squash formed the time-honoured seaside day-trip dinner, then maybe a paddle if it was warm enough, a doze in the sun, a stroll along the front and perhaps an ice cream or even a carton of cockles and whelks, and suddenly it was time to keep an eye on the clock. We'd leave the seaside in the late afternoon, for it took ages to get home with all the stops that took place along the way. Crates of beer weren't loaded on board when we set off and so at least one stop-off at a pub on the way back was considered essential, by the men at least. This was not as straightforward as it sounds, as by no means all pubs were willing or able to cater for coach parties; indeed they would either have signs up outside saying 'No Coaches' or 'Coaches Welcome'. After queuing for ages for the toilet, women would sit outside on benches in the garden, if there was one, with the children who weren't allowed into the pub itself. Women themselves were welcome inside if accompanied by a man, but they would usually settle the kids on a handy seat and go off to fetch lemonade and packets of crisps. The rest of the family were usually settled back on the coach when the men finally got back on board, usually after several pleas for them to do so. It was an exciting and satisfying end to a tiring day to call out 'good night' to friends and neighbours as the little groups dispersed and made their separate ways home through the dark and deserted streets, leaving the driver to take the coach back to the garage and then on at last to his own home.

Although there'd been a history of exchanges with French families earlier in the 1950s, there was no question of any of our class being taken anywhere for more than a few hours, let alone abroad. This could well have been because of the behaviour issue, but in retrospect it's more likely to have been because there were no suitable teachers to accompany us – partly because of their ages, partly because of the fact that the number of staff was so small that they couldn't be spared in term time.

Like us, there were no school holidays remembered from three other schools. The principal reasons elsewhere for venturing away from school were geography field trips, one of which was across the Thames to the Isle of Thanet. Weekends or weeks away, as well as outdoor activities in Hampshire in one case and Dorset in another, were arranged, both of them fairly local to the schools involved. By far the most cultural were the trips to London to see plays in Greek.

As for overseas holidays, at one school, where there were more than four times as many girls as we had, 'skiing trips were offered regularly. Once there was a summer cruise for those who could afford it. Otherwise it was just the dreaded language exchange visits.' At another, 'There was what our headmistress used to call the "Brest exchange" (to silent sniggers), but I don't remember anything else. I never went on a school trip anywhere.' Other girls were able to go on an 'exchange visit to Germany, age 14', their home town having recently acquired a German twin. However, 'many of us were homesick – it was our first visit abroad, two weeks was too long and we had not learnt any German', which was probably why it was less than successful. Elsewhere 'there were some overseas holidays. I went on one to Spain' and the boys and girls from a co-ed school went on 'A couple of trips to France. Others were offered but I didn't go.' Once again the same school that attended Greek plays in London topped the cultural list by taking its pupils on a cruise to classical sites in the Mediterranean.

When the summer holidays were over and we were back at school for the autumn term there were only a couple of distractions in the form of fairs and Bonfire Night (no Halloween then) before the festive season. At our particular school there were no celebration of any festivals as such; we may have sung one or two Advent hymns in assembly at the beginning of December but no decorations found their way into the classrooms and certainly no end-of-term production or party of any kind was organised. Unless you count the one unfortunate carol service in the village church at the end of our first term, the nearest we got to festivities was singing the Latin and French versions of a couple of hymns. In the 1960s Christmas didn't start until well into December, apart from Christmas cakes and puddings which had to be made in advance to allow them to mature. Traditionally this took place on stir-up Sunday, the one before Advent, although many people had the job taken care of well before then.

Christmas began in shop windows with glitter, tinsel, baubles and cotton wool artistically arranged into drifts, while labels reading 'Ideal Christmas Gift' were displayed on the most unlikely items. One speciality of the Traders' Association was the 'Spot the Mistake' competition. Contestants had to examine the window display carefully in order to discover an out of place item lurking in the window among the scarves, gloves, jewellery, compacts, picture frames, holly leaves, socks, aftershave and fake presents. This was not as easy as it sounds because so many of the shops stocked something of everything and everything or nothing looked out of place. There were even prizes offered for this feat of observation. Family-sized Christmas trees were freshly dug and their roots left on so that they could be put into larger pots outside or put into the garden afterwards. Some families dug up and replanted their trees year after year. There were some rather basic artificial trees made with tinsel or similar, but these took very much a subordinate position among the decorations.

Although we sighed and rolled our eyes when there was any mention of food shopping, it took a real knack to plan the seasonal menus and retain a careful balance between over-buying and being guilty of waste, or being seen as mean if there turned out to be a shortage of food. Without freezers, and very often without fridges, food could and did go off even if purchased at the very last minute. We never heard of anyone having goose for their Christmas dinner, and turkey was much less usual than a chicken or a capon. The vegetables were the same, but fresh from the market or local growers, not frozen, and gravy was made from stock and giblets, not just from cubes or granules (though these might still be added to give a boost). Christmas puds were generally home-made even though commercial ones were available, for they were a bit like fruit sponges and were over-sweet. For children, the best part about the pudding was the hope of finding one of the silver thrupenny bits (3d coins, which had been replaced by the twelve-sided brass one in 1942) or, even better, a sixpence.

Television programmes were very traditional, year in, year out. A real favourite was the seasonal ghost story, often on Christmas Eve, and most years there was at least one version of A Christmas Carol. Being in black and white, such programmes themselves were much more atmospheric than they are today and we were very much in the mood to be spooked. With no central heating, rooms were chilly and the open fire would throw strange moving shadows on to the walls and ceilings. The slightest noise – a moving coal or the cat scratching at the door to get out – would make your heart thump. The anticipation of knowing that the one of the ghosts would appear any second was nearly unbearable, and the scene where Scrooge reads his own name on the tombstone was very vivid.

On the day itself, broadcasts continued with church services and visits to children's hospitals in the morning, the Queen's Christmas message after lunch and in the evening a pantomime, usually with a star cast, and Christmas Night with the Stars. All too often the day ended with a dose of indigestion mixture; there was even a Christmas television commercial which went 'Eat, drink, and be merry, and don't forget the Alka-Seltzer'.

The festive season was different from today in that almost everywhere stayed closed on Boxing Day as well, because most workers went back to work on 27 December and then, very soon, another year had started.

Eleven

The Times they are A-Changin', Bob Dylan, 1964

The last day of term in July 1963 meant the end of an era for us for it was the last time that would all be together. As our history textbook told us, with reference to the ascension of Henry VII in 1485, *'tempora mutantur et nos mutamur in illis'*, that is, 'the times are changing and we change with them'. In 1960 Lionel Bart put it a tad more colloquially, 'fings ain't what they used t'be'.

The whole structure of our five years at grammar school had been geared towards O levels at the end. Very occasionally, pupils with special ability were allowed to take a subject at the end of the fourth year and quite a few people sat additional O levels alongside studying for A levels in the first year of sixth form. O levels had been introduced in England, Wales and Northern Ireland in 1951 and were the usual exams taken by grammar school pupils aged 16 years or so. They were not exclusive to grammar schools, however, for a number of high achievers in secondary modern schools also took them. The Certificate of Secondary Education (CSE) was a school-leaving qualification from 1965 to 1987, its Grade 1 being the equivalent of a pass at O level. In 1988 both O levels and CSEs were replaced by the GCSE (General Certificate of Secondary Education). Although they were abolished, O levels survived elsewhere in the English-speaking world.

The O level selection process began almost immediately once we got to grammar school, when we were divided for French classes. The final and greatest division was whether one went into upper or lower fifth, with their separate form rooms and curricula; put bluntly, upper was academic, lower, domestic. GCE A levels were also introduced in 1951 and until 2000 it was usual for pupils to take 3 A levels a couple of years after taking O levels. Both Os and As were set initially by twenty-nine examination boards (our school sat those of the Oxford Delegacy of Local Examinations); these later merged into five groups. The Oxford Locals were rumoured to be the 'easiest', which may have meant that the questions set were more easily understood by the minds of schoolchildren, rather than that the standard was lower.

It had been stated in the 1955 education report that in the fifth year 'any subject taught can be offered for examination and usually 7 or 8 are chosen'. The inspectors thought this might be 'rather too many subjects' and 'maybe lesser able pupils should be allowed to spread the work out over a longer period'. As is still usual, mock exams were set under exami-nation conditions and using questions from past papers. Each of our O level subjects was examined by sitting written papers (with aural and oral tests where appropriate), with no assignments or course work. If you were ill or had an off day when the time came to sit the exam, the entire five years' work was wasted. It was possible to retake but this set you back at least a term or, more frequently, the whole academic year. Retakes also carried a stigma, for grades obtained at a second sitting weren't seen as being of an equal status as those achieved the first time round.

Virtually everybody in our year had decided whether or not to go back to school after the summer holidays before they had even sat their O levels. As it was up to the school to say whether or not a girl was allowed to continue with a subject at A level if they'd done badly in their O level exam, dropping a grade or two was nowhere near as serious as it would later be at A level if applying to university. Those who would be teaching a pupil on her entry into the lower sixth would be aware of her progress throughout the school. One heartbreaking example in our class was a very able girl who had done well all the way until the fifth year, when she lost her mother at Christmas. Not surprisingly her schoolwork suffered and her O level results gave the impression that she was unsuitable grammar school material, when in reality this was very far from being the case.

According to their perceived ability, girls took anything from five to eight O levels and two or three A levels. If they were applying for Oxford or Cambridge they stayed on into a third-year sixth form, composed of only a couple of girls, where they prepared for the entry examinations.

Even today, when a grammar school pupil meets another who they don't know from their schooldays, sooner or later the conversation gets round to set books. The O levels which we took in the summer of 1963 were comparatively wide ranging. In addition to *Romeo and Juliet* and *The Nun's Priest's Tale*, the set books for English literature included George Elliot's *The Mill on the Floss*, which was generally disliked and gave at least one of us a lasting aversion to Elliot and all her works. An alternative was *Lark Rise to Candleford*, of which very few people had heard at that time, but which would doubtless have been much more appealing to us. It's odd to think that it has become such a popular television series nearly fifty years later.

The French syllabus didn't include any literature but more than made up for it by its oral and dictation sections. We were required to translate passages to and from French and to write an essay related to a series of drawings of the seaside (in which donkeys featured quite prominently). Latin, on the other hand, was very literature-orientated to compensate for its lack of oral or aural components. Translation was again to and from Latin, the study of J. Caesar's *De Gallic War* and Virgil's *Aeneid* as set books. The trials and tribulations of Aeneas and Co. left us cold; the war with Gaul, however, was much more to our taste, in particular Critognatus' proposal of cannibalism, which we found quite fascinating. One of our number was so horrified with what she read when she got to the questions on Virgil that her first thought was that there'd been some mistake and that the questions had been set on the wrong book. The error was, of course, entirely her own due to the fact that she'd been out and about on her boyfriend's motorbike instead of following the wanderings of Aeneas' party. She nearly passed out with shock and had to be escorted from the exam room to lie down. The school put in a request for her efforts to be given special consideration in view of her having been 'unwell' during the exam, but this was judged to be unnecessary as what she had already written before the horror of the Virgil had earned her a Grade 3. This was, of course, a huge compliment to Bessie's teaching of the subject.

The human biology & hygiene paper came up to expectations with the anticipated and well-rehearsed questions on the alimentary canal, the human reproductive system (was it the male or female that year?) and the life history of the house fly, including its shortcomings in general and its propensity to poo and puke on foodstuffs in particular. The remaining subjects were judged to be fair (although maths proved a bit of a stumbling block as usual) so, all in all, there was no real cause for complaint.

The results came out towards the end of August as duplicated copies sealed up safely inside the stamped, addressed envelopes, which we'd had to bring to school and leave in the office before we left for the summer break. There was no rushing off to school to look at lists pinned up for public viewing, and of course no texting. If we wanted to know how our classmates had got on we had two options, asking them outright or waiting to see the results as published in the local paper for the delectation of an even wider readership.

The number of girls sitting O levels for the first time that year was a total of thirty-one, of whom twenty were in the upper and eleven in the lower fifth. The local paper also listed seventeen girls from the form above who had added to their initial number of passes, showing that at this period O levels had some importance in their own right. Grades do not seem to have been of paramount importance unless one intended to go on to A level or specialise. The greatest number of subjects passed was nine, the least three.

Passes in English language were 100 per cent and there were only two failures in English literature – one of which was not surprising for this girl had consistently got low grades and was the person with only three passes, the other was the girl who had recently lost her mother. It will be remembered that both English exams were taken by everybody in the class which reflects very well on Auntie Dottie's ability to get the best out of us. It's difficult to compare these successes in English with those in other subjects because, apart from geography, which also had a high pass rate, other subjects weren't compulsory. However, in the sciences eleven girls passed general science and eleven biology, as well as the eight (nearly all from the lower fifth) who passed human biology & hygiene, which indicates that only one person failed to obtain a pass in any scientific subject.

In the same edition of the paper under the heading 'Congratulations' can be seen a message to a girl at the nearby city grammar school. It is from 'Mummy, Daddy, David and Julia'. If any one of us had been the recipient of such an announcement we'd have curled up and died of embarrassment. The boys' results were published the same week and were similar to our own.

By 1955 about a fifth of those who left after O levels went on to further education or training, including two girls who had got into university, eleven to teacher training and fourteen to nursing-related jobs. One career suggestion made to us was nursery nursing, which proved that the speaker had no experience of us personally for you'd have been wiser to employ King Herod than anybody in our year. Even those isolated cases who were of a kindly or maternal disposition (and there were none that spring to mind immediately) would have had more than enough of that sort of thing at home, and looked on a grammar school education as a way of escaping it.

At the prize-giving in 1958, the year that we arrived, Miss D. had criticised the fifth-form O level results when only 39 per cent of the girls had passed five or more subjects, which was 20 per cent down on the previous year. 'This reflects the inability of some girls to learn thoroughly and their careless and inaccurate approach to their work,' she said, and added that the co-operation of parents was essential. The results of our own O levels in 1963 showed that 84 per cent of us got five or more O levels at the first attempt, which cheered Daisy up somewhat. She still insisted that staying on to take A levels would mean a wider selection of better-paid and more rewarding jobs, but once again, the encouragement of the parents was necessary. The odds were stacked against this happening, however. Little had changed since the 1955 education report had stated that there was 'No history or expectations of girls staying on after 15 or 16 at latest'. The inspectors expressed the hope that in the future many more will stay on into the lower sixth; 'even if they still go on later to relatively humble and unambitious occupations'. At the time when we left school, and for some considerable time afterwards, women were automatically paid less than men even if they were doing the same jobs.

In regard to our own class, some had jobs to go to and others were leaving to go into further (as opposed to higher) education. For teenage girls at this time one of the most attractive training courses at technical colleges was hairdressing, although by far most female school-leavers with O levels went on to learn secretarial skills or bookkeeping. A few people stayed on for a further year to take more O levels but didn't go on into the upper sixth afterwards. Four people did so from our class, adding art, human biology or religious knowledge to their first batch of O levels. Seven others added variations of these three subjects and then went on to do A levels. In all, there were thirteen girls in the upper sixth in the academic year 1964/65 and they obtained twenty-six A levels between them, the most popular being English literature (seven) and French (three), with only one in Latin, and that without French. Only two girls passed in three subjects, the rest in two and, in one case, only one subject. Of those who went on to further study, one went to train as a sports teacher and the rest to Welsh, redbrick or new universities.

The 1955 report was confident that the 'needs of potential university entrants were catered for', but this was not strictly true. The school's first university graduate gained an honours degree in English at Exeter University in 1956. There was an honours board above the fireplace in the hall, but by the early 1960s there were only a few names on it, and those mainly to redbrick universities. Previous years had sent the occasional girl to Oxford and Cambridge, but this was very much the exception.

On discussing A level results and applying to university, a former head girl revealed that she wasn't made aware of the fact that a clearing system existed. If someone failed to achieve the required grades, that appeared to be that; the end of a possible academic career. In the fifth year we had been given no advice about what O levels to choose or drop, and what the effects might be both initially in regard to doing A levels, and long term to university and beyond. Remarks were made to members of the upper fifth who declined to stay on into the lower sixth, saying that they wanted to get out into the real world and earn their own money and settle down to get married. These comments were to the effect that education was never wasted and (a cheerful thought) that if the school-leaver was ever to become a widow (or, heaven forbid, a divorcee), they might need their education to get a job to support any hypothetical children of the marriage. One or two cynics were heard to remark that head teachers must be well paid per head of pupils, in the way that doctors were paid for patients registered with their practice. Very few people realised that keeping up the numbers was essential for the school to stay open at all, so it must have been gratifying to Miss D. to be able to announce that the number of pupils had increased from 134 in its first year to 184 in 1958. An anonymous account of the first eight years of the school (1949–57) confides that having left school 'girls have taken up various trades and professions. These include court-dressmaking, cartography, and university educations leading to a wide range of professions, as well as the more usual teaching, nursing, banking and secretarial work.'

In 1959 the prizes were presented by the head of one of the Oxford women's colleges, who told the girls that they should find out which careers they were most needed in, as well as what they'd most enjoy. Both nursing and teaching, for instance, needed a supply of educated young women. It was all very well for head teachers and prize-day speakers to hold forth on the subject of staying on at school past the minimum leaving age, but economic considerations played an extremely important part in such decisions. In some cases there was no question of the girls staying on longer than they had to, especially if there were several academically minded children in the family. Nevertheless, the desirability of staying on into at least the lower sixth was the recurring theme of Miss D.'s address to the school, year in, year out. In 1956 she said she was particularly glad about the increasing number of girls in the sixth form:

> ... the fullest benefits of a grammar school education are not to be derived until a girl has had the valuable experience that membership of the sixth form can give. It is by the deeper and more scholarly study of subjects in which she has a particular interest that a girl learns to develop that capacity for independent thought and logic reasoning that will enable her in adult life to form an unprejudiced judgement.

She was concerned that more girls were taking Saturday and holiday jobs as, while not a bad thing in itself, it meant less leisure time for reading and thought. However, she did concede that some had to take jobs so that they could stay on at school. She hoped that in the future allowances for this would be made so that these jobs would be no longer necessary. It seems to have totally escaped most people at the time that women and girls needed a certain amount of financial independence, whatever the family's income. In the early 1960s, pocket money was supplemented by jobs in family businesses, as dogsbodies in local shops and, for an adventurous few, working in Woolworth's in town.

In 1958 we were told that a girl would have to make the best of the fact that when she was in the fifth form, her contemporaries would be out in the big world earning their own money. This was not something that we wanted to be reminded about. The advice was to leave after the fifth only if you wanted to do something positive such as nursery nursing, catering or secretarial work. The following year Miss D. confided that yet again she felt a real disappointment about the fact that gifted girls were leaving after O levels. Admittedly it was possible to work and study but, she stressed, 'studying while working is a long and arduous process, and it is not in the interests of either the girl or the nation'. Another year she announced that she found it distressing that high wages lured youth away from education, indeed:

> ... so many give way to the restlessness of adolescence and the lure of high wages. Industry, not content with taking practically all the science graduates, is now taking arts graduates and training them in their scientific methods so that it looks as if English, history, etc may soon be added to the list of subjects in which it is almost impossible to get a teacher.

This sounds strange today when arts graduates are finding it increasingly difficult to find employment and some of their subjects are even classed as 'self-indulgent'.

We appear to be in the minority in regard to the number of girls who left after the fifth form in comparison with other grammar schools of that period, although some schools did have leavers who went into secretarial jobs and shops and offices. One pupil from a nearby girls' grammar said, 'I don't know if any went to university, possibly one or two.' Approximately half of the O level year at one school went on to do A levels; those who left went into nursing, office work, banking and hairdressing. At another: 'I suspect that employment was very varied.'

According to a school magazine, of the fifty-six girls in the two fifth-form groups in one year, thirteen left after O levels. The contributor commented:

> One got married immediately as she was pregnant, but I have no idea what the other twelve leavers did. They probably went into banks and the like, as you did not need A-levels for this kind of work then.

Similarly:

> We didn't know at the end of the fifth form whether people were coming back or not: we were only allowed to come back and take A-levels if we achieved Grades 1–3 in the subjects we wanted to study at the Oxford Local Examinations at O-level.

> I went on to do my nursery nursing certificate (instead of finishing my A-levels) before going to Teacher Training College.

You could count the number who left after 'O'-levels on one hand. I don't know what they went on to do!'

Hardly anyone left another school so early, and at another:

I can't remember anyone leaving after 'O' levels although there must have been some. Most stayed on to do 'A' levels. [Going on to university was] almost inevitable.

About a quarter went into 6th form and then University. Of those who left, one girl started her own business (still going strong), Armed Forces, a Charity, Post Office, Bank and working for parents' business. From asking around my friends, most seem to have gone to white collar jobs.

Most progressed to Sixth Form [and] of those who stayed on, most of them went to college or university.

Of the 43 or so sixth-formers in my year, 16 went to university, 1 to medical school, 9 to colleges of education, and 4 to nursing training. The other 13 did not do anything that the school thought worth recording in the school magazine. Some of them may have done some kind of training, so it is probably safe to say that nearly two-thirds did further education.

At the most academic end of the scale:

… it was expected that girls from TGGS would go on to university. The vast majority did.

Anyone who did not go to university was considered a failure, and it must have grieved the headmistress that a number of girls with three As at A-level chose to go to training college instead.

Another high-achieving school sent girls 'to Oxbridge every year, and many other universities'.

Of those who left another school in this book after the fifth form:

Some went into secretarial jobs, but the likelihood of leavers going on to further education, including training was quite high. There were County Major Scholarships to University, art school, teacher training, etc.

The pupil who contributed this information came back to her old school and worked her way up to be head of games there. Lastly, her husband, an old boy of Lord Bill's, reported that their prospects were even better, indeed 'Excellent, especially to Oxbridge and the ancient red-bricks'.

It was not unknown for parents to find their daughters jobs and inform them of the fact only after arrangements had been finalised. As late as 1963, one was told by her father that she was to start at one of the local banks in a few days time. When she protested that she didn't think that she'd be happy there, she was told in no uncertain terms that 'you go to work to earn your living, not to enjoy yourself'. It wasn't until after he died that she learnt her father had been an exemplary pupil at a very well-considered grammar school, winning form and sub-ject prizes and matriculating for university. When his mother was diagnosed with cancer, he had to give up any hope he'd had in that direction and get himself a job in the Post Office, a job which he'd disliked all his life. Apparently, thirty-five years afterwards, his sudden transformation from the blue-eyed baby of the family to joint breadwinner still rankled.

Lastly, as a counterbalance to what grammar school girls were doing with their lives in the 1950s and '60s, here's what the eleven secondary modern pupils that were asked for their views have achieved: one became a town mayor; another a district councillor; two became justices of the peace; one president of the local British Legion; two chair of Townswomen's Guild; one emigrated and became an accountant; two were Girl Guide district commissioners; one the chairman of Town in Bloom; one a trustee of a museum; one a member of Conservation Advisory Committee; one became a nurse; one a teacher; one a hairdresser; one a company director; one completed an engineering apprenticeship; and one became a reader in the Roman Catholic Church and read at the English College in Rome. This is certainly a very creditable list of achievements for pupils who had been written off as no-hopers in the 1950s and '60s, just because they failed the Eleven Plus and so didn't come to join us at grammar school.

Twelve

Us and Them, Pink Floyd, 1973

The overall picture created by responses from grammar school girls is that they realised that they were privileged and, as such, under an obligation to make the most of the opportunities which had been offered them. There is little indication that they considered themselves personally superior to secondary modern pupils, many of whom had been their friends at primary school. It was the education at grammar school that was better academically, and not necessarily the social class of the pupils – although of course this sometimes proved to be the case in the long term.

When asked for their views on the advantages and drawbacks of a grammar school education reactions varied considerably:

I thought it was brilliant. Managed properly – without this ridiculous farce of parental choice, false catchment areas, bad funding management, and the perception that a technical education is somehow poorer than an academic one – the selective system should provide everyone with the best education, tailored to their particular skills and aptitudes. The grammar school system really did provide opportunities for the less-well-off to receive an education equal to that in a public school.

I'm 100% in favour of grammar schools. There was a good social mix of all backgrounds and income. Everyone was treated exactly the same and any snobbery from wealthier pupils was soon dealt with. A good education was not about how much money you had or whether your parents encouraged you. Those who wanted and needed an academic education got it, standards were set and you were expected and encouraged to rise to the challenge. If you didn't or couldn't, there was always someone to help you. As my sister went to a Secondary Modern I can say that she flourished there because she was given the choice of academic or practical subjects. My horizons were certainly widened and it opened up a whole new world for me. It also gave me self confidence, self respect and the knowledge that with hard work I could achieve more than had been expected.

It worked for me. As ever, it was dependent on quality of teachers and head-teacher leadership. Discipline was much better than in larger comprehensive that followed … More encouraging of academic achievement.

… a better experience than the comprehensive, with good teaching and being more competitive.

As for any drawbacks:

… none as far as I was concerned. It was an excellent school. Scholarships were available for the academically able so that it was not 'elitist'.

No drawbacks at all, my thoughts at the time were that I was lucky in that I could see all sorts of possibilities up for grabs. Secondary modern teaching was 'basic' and at that time further education was not an option.

… excellent academically although teaching of 'life skills' could have been improved. I think that had more to do with the nuns than the fact that it was a grammar school. The classes were small.

[Grammar schools] don't always teach subjects that will help with future employment.

The only person who had an unpleasant time at a grammar school said that it offered 'a good academic education, but was in every other way a disaster'. In view of the experiences that this pupil had during her time there, this reaction is hardly surprising, but fortunately it is very much in the minority.

The only male respondent stated that he was 'totally split down the middle: I was fortunate to have a privileged education, but spent the whole of my working life compensating for it'. This turned out to be relative to working at firstly a secondary modern and then a comprehensive school. Other descriptions were:

Us and Them. Pink Floyd. 1973

A positive stepping-stone on the way to College – but my
self-confidence was not particularly built because we were
never actually told 'Well done'.

… perhaps there was rather a lot of pressure on people
who were not really academic but had passed the
Scholarship. However, it did make you work and have a
positive approach to the future.

I did not enjoy school but I appreciated the quality of my
education, both at the time and subsequently. We were
given a solid grounding in a standard range of subjects
and were expected to be able to think for ourselves. In retrospect, this also meant learning self-discipline. A current
friend refers to this as the grammar school ethos, which
also produced a straightforward and honest approach to
conducting oneself. It could be said that much of the curriculum was not apparently relevant to everyday life nor
seemed to have a practical application, but over the years I
have used what I learnt at school in the wider cultural con-
text of life. In particular, I appreciate having learnt Latin,
which has been invaluable for understanding language,
history, culture and so much more. The general benefits of
grammar school education were so important to me that
I battled hard to get my daughter into a grammar school.

One thing is without doubt, however much girls liked or
disliked their schooldays they're united in stating that educational standards were high.

Like our attitude to teachers at grammar schools, at the
time we had no idea of the sacrifices which might have
been made by our parents and condemned anyone who
didn't want (or in a few cases didn't allow) their child to go

to grammar school. Apart from the considerable expense involved, many parents feared that their offspring might be bullied, ignored or patronised by their schoolmates. If they had had little contact with the middle classes they sometimes viewed them with suspicion and had no wish for their own children to copy them and become 'la-di-dah'. Worse still, they might grow to look down on their own families and be ashamed of being seen with them.

Fathers' occupations at our school seem very much in line with those countrywide, in that they included manual and agricultural workers, farmers and smallholders, owners of shops and small businesses, a fish-and-chip shop proprietor, clerks and office workers, police officers, armed services, civil servants, local government, teachers (including at least three headmasters), clergymen, a bank manager, a university lecturer and an MP. Some schools, such as Cheney, reflected local employment and included lots of workers at the car factory. Not surprisingly, in view of the fact that virtually all the children came from small 'ordinary' schools, privilege is not a word which could be applied to their fathers' backgrounds. The only possible contender was a long-serving MP and government minister who was knighted in 1979. His daughter was created a baroness by the Labour government. The Lord Bill's boys could boast that 'because of the school's proximity to Oxford, there were academics; the boarding side brought in service families as well as internationally-acclaimed actors'.

Mothers' incomes, if any, were looked on as pin-money and were usually gained from family businesses or part-time shop work and seldom mentioned. Women still, as in Jane Austen's novels, acquired their husbands' status at marriage.

The proportion of those girls who had one or both parents with a grammar school education varied considerably.

A few were first-generation grammar school and had other siblings at a secondary modern. Others had family at a range of schools from public to private and grammar, despite the fact that their parents hadn't been to any of these. One or two even went to the same grammar school that their mothers had attended.

The girls' statements as to how they saw themselves are surprisingly diverse and some are worth quoting verbatim. From the positive to the negative, they are:

Certainly privileged as most of us came from what would now be described as a deprived area. Also we were proud to be going to a school with such a rich history and good reputation. It was the pupils at the Secondary Modern schools who seemed to feel inferior to us and let us know! Certainly the ethos of the school was NOT to be superior. Neighbours were very proud that someone from 'their' street had passed the 11 plus and would, they hoped, go on to achieve more than they had themselves. Especially as that year as at our local school half of the class passed the 11 plus. Most adults in the area would ask how we were doing and encourage us to work hard.

Other complimentary comments were 'privileged and very proud of the school', 'privileged and a little superior, it was a good school', 'certainly superior to the neighbouring comprehensive' and 'relieved to have got to Grammar School'.

In regard to not feeling superior: 'No, because the bright girls went to the High School; we did however feel superior to the technical school next door', 'I don't think we viewed ourselves as particularly special. I suppose that we knew we were academically brighter than people in other schools, but we didn't feel superior as a result.'

Intelligence was more relevant than social class to the pupil who wrote:

> I think we all realised that we were in the top 20% (or what-ever the figure was) as you had to pass the 11 plus to get there. I particularly felt the difference as my sisters didn't make it to grammar school. I hated being called 'brainy'.

The chance of a sound education was valued by one pupil who stated, 'I'm not sure that we thought about it except that we knew it was a very good academic environment'. The pupil who had been at two grammar schools felt 'normal', whilst one had 'No feelings either way'. A sad note was introduced with the girl who'd felt 'Not privileged or supe-rior; it was where one went if one passed the 11+', although 'Yes – we were viewed as special! It broke up friendships made at Junior School.'

Once again the most negative feelings were from the same pupil, who felt:

> Hard-done by, overworked, and underprivileged. We certainly weren't proud to be at the school. Going to a grammar school meant complete alienation from all my primary school friends, as no one where I lived went with me. A constant dilemma was do I take my hat off and break the school rules (a terrible sin), or do I keep it on and get it knocked off and possibly stolen by former friends? We were regarded as snobs and potential victims.

Someone who'd been at three different grammar schools and later became a head teacher at a primary school criticised the grammar school because 'It was socially divisive. We were the elite but all the others were classed as failures at the age of 11.'